REVISED AND EXPANDI

HELP

FOR THE

Helpmeet ™

BECOMING THE HELPMEET GOD
CREATED FOR YOUR HUSBAND

YVETTE BENTON

Help for the Helpmeet: Becoming the Helpmeet God Created for Your Husband

Revised and Expanded Edition

Help for The Helpmeet, Inc.

Kennesaw, GA

Assisted by Scribe Empire, LLC

Cover Design by Angela Mills Camper of Dezign Pro Printing & Graphics

Revised Edition 2023

ISBN: 978-1-7346335-5-9

I dedicate this book to my amazing and anointed Priest, Prophet &
King (PPK), Apostle Gerald Benton Jr. The man who knew and
declared I would be his wife from the moment he met me in high
school. That declaration put a demand in Heaven. We survived the
worst of times in our marriage journey. Through God's delivering
power and hard work, we have been blessed with a "do over" many
never experience. Thank you for all you have done to restore our
family. I love you unconditionally and honor you. I am so proud to be
your Helpmeet SUITABLE!

CONTENTS

ACKNOWLEDGMENTS

I want to thank our children for sharing me with the world. It is not easy being a transparent preacher's child. Your dad and I love you so much. I thank my family for their love and support during our difficult separations and challenges. To our spiritual sons and daughters, mentees and members of Impart Ministries International, thank you for trusting the God in us. We love the covenant family God is building. We will continue to keep marriage, ministry and marketplace in God's divine order!

INTRODUCTION

For years, women have been asking, "Where are all the good men?" Let me respond by saying, "Where are all the good Helpmeets?" Although families, churches, and communities seldom discuss it, being a Helpmeet is a role God takes very seriously. Therefore, if you're already married, being a Helpmeet is one of your most important assignments. If you are not married and desire to be married, then your future Husband is looking for you. Future Helpmeets should be actively preparing themselves by studying the role and healing from past hurts.

There are hundreds of books, articles, podcasts, videos, tapes, workbooks, and magazines on weddings and being a bride or wife. You name it—it's out there. Unfortunately, there are limited resources available to uncover the job and responsibilities of a Helpmeet. To fill that void, this book will walk you through the important role of a Helpmeet.

Reflecting on the journey of deliverance for my Husband and me, as well as our marriage, I made a vow to both God and my Husband to be more than just a wife. Anybody can be a wife, but it takes a submitted and obedient woman with specialized training to be a Helpmeet Suitable.

By no means am I the perfect Helpmeet but because God gave me the job, I work hard at it.

Teaching about the role and responsibilities of a Helpmeet was birthed from the pain and frustration in our marriage and the revelation we were experiencing tough times. It was refined when I was counseling and praying with women who believed in God for their Husbands, future Husbands, marriages, and families. I am happy to serve in this capacity because I know what the revelation has done for my marriage. As my Husband and I tell the world about how good God is, we have to share our testimony. God not only delivered my Husband from lust, perversion, drugs, and deception but also, so much more. He delivered me from anger, bitterness, unforgiveness, and being judgmental. Through this journey, I learned that it wasn't my job to judge but to be the Helpmeet God created for my Husband. I pray my pain has a purpose, and marriages can be saved and restored through the revelation and wisdom imparted by the Holy Spirit.

1

IN THE BEGINNING...

*"Now the Lord God said, 'It is not good (sufficient,
satisfactory) that the man should be alone; I will
make him a helper meet [suitable, adaptable and
complimentary] for him'" (Genesis 2:18 AMPC).*

"In the beginning, God created the heavens and the earth"
(Genesis 1:1). God created man soon after He made His
other creations. After designing the man, He saw it fit to
form the woman out of the man. As I studied Genesis Chapter 2, it
was eye-opening to read that God called everything "good" until He
created Adam. In Genesis 2:18, God said, "It is not good (sufficient,
satisfactory) that the man should be alone; I will make him a helper
meet (suitable, adaptable and complementary) for him." In this verse,
we observe that God recognized a need and fulfilled it by creating a
helper for Adam. This helper had to be complementary to Adam
before God would declare him "good." It goes against God's nature
to leave His creations lacking, so He fashioned the woman to
balance and complete Adam. I thought to myself, "This is such a

monumental task!" It was a task that pleased God so greatly that it left a deep impression on my heart, compelling me to study and present myself approved for such an assignment.

As I continued to study, I asked myself, "Am I suitable? Am I adaptable? Am I complementary?" I realized I had to be honest with myself, and I could not decide if I was any of those things. Therefore, I not only needed to seek God for answers, but I also asked my Husband how I was doing in these areas. It's important to consistently seek guidance from God and get our Husbands' feedback to assess whether we're suitable and adept as Helpmeets. As Helpmeets, we must inquire of God whether we're suitable for the current season in our Husbands' lives. As we journey through different seasons, our needs and desires shift.

When I first asked God about my role as my Husband's Helpmeet, I was surprised by His response. This occurred during a challenging period in our marriage when I blamed my Husband for our difficulties. I felt incapable of being a better wife. Honestly, I was fulfilling my wife's role, but was it truly the role of a Helpmeet? I maintained my commitment, remained faithful, managed household tasks, cared for our children, and had a successful career. From my perspective, my Husband was fortunate to have me. It might sound prideful, but that's how I truly felt. So, you can understand why I was taken aback when I heard God's response to what I believed was "good."

I began, willing and prepared to listen. What I heard from Him was very different. Reality struck me. I was mistaken. God wasn't satisfied with how "I" was handling things. He held a different perspective on what a Helpmeet Suitable for my Husband should be like. The Holy Spirit became my guide, and I learned my role as Helpmeet. I was meant to respect my Husband, assist him in areas where he needed help, and love him unconditionally with God's love, regardless of his actions. Yes, you read that correctly. This concept was new to me, as it might be to you. I had no idea about God's plans for me. I did know, however, that God wasn't merely going to address my Husband; He intended to work with me too.

SUITABLE, ADAPTABLE, AND COMPLEMENTARY

According to the Oxford dictionary, the word "suitable" means right or appropriate for a person, purpose, or situation. The definition of "adaptable" is to be able to adjust to new conditions and be capable of being modified for a new use or purpose. "Complementary" means combining in a way that enhances or emphasizes the qualities of another. After reading these definitions, what comes to mind? A Helpmeet! You are correct.

A Helpmeet must learn these terms and know how to operate with these very attributes. Although it's a challenging task, it is extremely critical. This task often takes us out of our comfort zones. What if your Husband needs something today that he has never needed before? What would you do in a situation like this? Being in daily communion with the Holy Spirit is imperative. Why? Because the Holy Spirit is the one who teaches and guides you in unfamiliar seasons. When God was addressing this topic with me, the Holy Spirit said, "You're the helper." The Helpmeet is the representative of the Holy Spirit in your marital union.

For those who are unmarried, I encourage you to study the Holy Spirit and ask Him to commune with you. Allow Him to prepare you to be a representative for Him. Current Helpmeets—ask God for forgiveness for doing it your way and to reveal His way to you. Ask God to show you how to be suitable, adaptable, and complementary to your Husband.

HELPMEET JOURNAL ENTRY

1. What is God saying to you after reading this chapter?
2. What prayer targets do you need to add?

~

_____
_____
_____
_____
_____
_____
_____
_____
_____
_____
_____
_____
_____
_____
_____
_____
_____
_____
_____
_____
_____

_____
_____
_____
_____
_____
_____
_____
_____
_____
_____
_____
_____
_____
_____
_____
_____
_____
_____
_____
_____
_____
_____
_____
_____
_____
_____
_____
_____

2
MARRIAGE

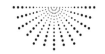

As Helpmeets, we must learn to master marriage, ministry, and mindset. If these are not fully understood, we cannot truly operate in our Helpmeet roles. The role of the Helpmeet is not just in marriage, but it's a mindset, a Kingdom principle. Being a Helpmeet is part of God's design, outlined in His Word. Therefore, we need to shift how we perceive marriage and ministry, adopting the Helpmeet perspective and aligning it with God's perspective.

The Bible instructs us in Isaiah 55:9 that God's ways and thoughts surpass ours. Consequently, we must establish a solid foundation for the Helpmeet role and elevate our thinking. Our aim is to consistently operate within the role that God has ordained for us as Helpmeets.

When God formed us in our mothers' wombs, He created us to be Helpmeets, and He has expectations for us. His expectations hold significance because how can we teach our daughters if we have no expectations? How can we serve as examples to the body of Christ and to those who heed our voices if we don't truly comprehend God's expectations of us? We must grasp the Helpmeet role biblically, articulate it, and make it a part of our lives. We must become a prototype of this and set an example on Earth. The Kingdom of God needs to restore the family, and understanding the Helpmeet role will aid us in fulfilling these expectations.

I often say to Helpmeets, "Create an atmosphere that is conducive for your Priest, Prophet, and King to feel respected, honored, and loved unconditionally." I call my Husband my Priest, Prophet, and King because I learned through my journey that I didn't understand my Husband's role. My lack of understanding about who he was made it challenging for me to create a suitable atmosphere for him. I had to understand who he was to create an atmosphere conducive to who God created him to be. Part of my lack of understanding was that I didn't know who God created me to be. Our Husbands operate as the Priests of their homes, bringing their families before God. They also operate as the Prophets of their homes, not necessarily holding the title of a Prophet, but being able to speak things into existence concerning their families. Our Husbands also operate as the Kings of their homes as they are called to govern their households appropriately.

God expects us to respond and behave in a certain way. When these expectations become an integral part of your active lifestyle, you will see the principles reflected in everything you do. They will manifest in your role as a mother, a woman of God, and even a child. These principles will operate effectively in every area of your life. Therefore, we must remove the stigma that being a Helpmeet is only for married people. If I had learned how to be a Helpmeet when I got married, my entire marriage would have been different. My children would be different, and I know that for a fact. My finances would have been different as well. Hence, I am here to convey that being a Helpmeet transcends marriage; it is a Kingdom principle. The Bible tells us in Proverbs 4:7 that wisdom is the principal thing; therefore, we must seek wisdom. Wisdom can take on different forms for different people. Without it, we will not be able to fully operate in the Helpmeet role, so we must be those who seek the wisdom of God. Scripture serves as the foundation for our wisdom. As Kingdom women, delivered individuals, and those who are healed and set free, many of us will need to undo the traditions and culture that we have learned and witnessed throughout our lives. We must seek the Lord for a biblical understanding of what He expects from us as Helpmeets. Our personal opinions must be set aside. We need to remain open to receiving godly revelations. Closing our spiritual minds will hinder us from receiving such revelations. As a result, we will default to what we know, what we've always done, and rely on our feelings.

HELPMEET DEFINITIONS

So, let's take a look at the definition of a Helpmeet. The Greek word for Helpmeet is *ezer* (ay' - zer). This is from the Greek word meaning "to aid or to help." When God speaks to you and asks you to do something, and you realize He's addressing you as aid or help, you gain a better understanding of why you need to follow His request and the perspective from which He's speaking. During my journey, as God began speaking to me, I didn't fully comprehend His instructions until I understood His perception of me and how He created me.

When strangers speak to me, they won't say or expect certain things. However, if my daddy speaks to me, I know he's talking to me as a daughter, so his words, perceptions, and expectations are different.

Similarly, when we speak to our children, it's different from addressing a stranger's child because we see our children as our own.

When God gave me instructions, my lack of understanding led to disobedience. I disregarded what He said and talked myself out of it until I realized He was guiding me because He created me to be a Helpmeet. From the beginning, God called me to be a help, so I now understand that His instructions originate from that position and posture.

The Merriam-Webster dictionary defines the word Helpmeet as one who is a companion and helper, especially the wife. You can use the word Helpmeet or Helpmate. I specifically use the term Helpmeet because when I was on my knees begging God to help me and seeking Him for answers, He began to give me revelations. Many of you know my Husband's and my story—our marriage was utterly broken, a complete mess. So many things were going on, and I would tell God, "I'm a good wife. Why is all of this happening to me?" I was pleading with God for revelation and insight. I would remind God that I'm a good person; I studied His word, attended church, am a pastor, and a good wife. Then, God very intently said to me, "Yvette, you are a good wife, but you are not a Helpmeet and you are not suitable." That shook me because I thought they were the same but clearly, they are not. God said, "You can operate as a wife. There are certain things that you can do that wives do, and you are doing the majority of those things, but when you are a Helpmeet, you realize I created you to help your Husband." The Lord began to tell me that if I understood that He put certain things inside me to help my Husband, I would understand how to be a Helpmeet Suitable. This changed everything for me. I thought it changed my marriage, but honestly, it transformed my relationship with God. It changed the way I studied. It changed the way I pursued things. It transformed my family, my children, and is now genuinely my legacy. It is a ministry. This is where I am passionate about helping others, and I wish I had that realization much earlier because I know my life would be different.

So let's understand some synonyms for the term "Helpmeet." Some of the synonyms I like to use are: helper, adjunct, adjutant, aid, apprentice, lieutenant, assistant, and mate. We are joined to our Husbands, and our purpose is to support them. We are to be their lieutenants. I encourage you, as an assignment and strategy, to start looking up words and terms that mean "to help" or "to assist" that resonate with you. You must discover the terms that personally inspire you. The words that are effective for me might not be for you, but your goal is to make this your lifestyle and to shift your mindset. Therefore, you'll need to put in the effort and search for synonyms in the dictionary, which you should keep easily accessible. This journey is about personalization, so find the terms that work for you and your Husband. As an example, my Husband and I, both enthusiastic sports fans, started using the term "assistant head coach," which improved our understanding. This perspective helped my Husband realize that he is the head coach of the family. In the beginning, he didn't understand Priest, Prophet, and King, it sounded too deep but when I said, "Honey, you're the head coach of the family," he understood that and it worked for us at first.

It's crucial to understand what God said about the Helpmeet role. If you don't remind yourself about it then you may not be as convinced or convicted to operate in it. There is no marriage, man, or circumstance on the face of the earth that will enable you to function in this role effectively and consistently other than God. The only way you will fully operate in this calling is to realize that God said it in His Word, so God expects it. God called you to it. If you try to fulfill this role for a person, then the moment that person does something that bothers, hurts, or frustrates you, you may retreat from the role and displease God. Let's take a look at what the Word of God says concerning this Helpmeet role.

"Now the Lord God said, It is not good (sufficient, satisfactory) that the man should be alone; I will make him a helper (suitable, adapted, complementary) for him" (Genesis 2:18 AMPC).

"Now the Lord God said, "It is not good (beneficial) for the man to be alone; I will make him a helper [one who balances him—a counterpart who is] suitable and complementary for him" (Genesis 2:18 AMP).

I've been studying this role for 10-12 years, and it happened in the midst of a struggle for me. My Husband and I went through reconciliation and restoration, and then God chose to use us in ministry. I am still seeking understanding, knowledge, and hearing what God is saying concerning this. So, I want to encourage you that it takes continual study of God's Word. Some people may think that because they've read the book and tried the principles, it's immediately going to all stick, but anything that we do for the Lord requires that we progress in levels from glory to glory. It's like when we first get saved; we don't assume that we have all the faith we need right away for everything God asks us to do. We must study to show ourselves approved. We may grasp one level of revelation concerning this Helpmeet role but not the full understanding all at once, so it is a journey and a process.

I encourage you not to give up on the study of this role. It's comparable to having a job and thinking that because you hold the title, you don't need to go to work anymore or learn new software, new laws, or new ways of dealing with people. This kind of thinking would be flawed, as excelling in any job requires continuous learning. It's a process that deserves respect.

Consider it this way: How often do you read the Word of God and come across a scripture you've seen many times before; yet, in your new season and with your growing understanding, you read the same verse and gain an entirely new revelation? We've all experienced that. So, I am encouraging you not to let the enemy make you feel discouraged about having to keep revisiting this role. We have to keep revisiting it because it's a lifestyle. We have to keep coming back to gain deeper revelations.

I use the Amplified Classic Version (AMPC) and the Amplified Version (AMP) for the verse we looked at in Genesis 2:18, but you can use whichever version you prefer. Genesis 2:18 is the foundation of our study on the Helpmeet role. This version is what helped me understand what God meant when He told me that I was a good wife, but I was not a Helpmeet. As I began my study, this is what helped me comprehend what God was asking of me. It is imperative to understand that it is the Lord speaking in this verse. It is not Adam asking for something. This is the Lord saying something, and that has to carry significance for us. At the beginning of the book of Genesis, we see that this is where God had been breathing life and creating things into existence. Previously, what God had spoken into existence and created, He declared as good. But now, in Genesis 2:18, we see that the Lord God said, "It is not good." We must grasp the magnitude of God saying that something is not good, because this is the first time we encounter in Scripture where God calls something not good. The AMPC version of this verse says it's not sufficient and not satisfactory. Therefore, God is expressing that He did something, but it's not sufficient for man to be alone. If Adam, in all his closeness to God, wasn't good being alone, neither is it good for your Husband to be alone.

God has made us helpers to meet our Husbands' needs. He has designed us to be individuals who are suitable, adaptable, and complementary. I've highlighted the word "adaptable" because that's how I heard it. You've got to adapt as a Helpmeet. You can't just be suitable in one season and not realize your Priest, Prophet, and King has different seasons. Not only do we need to adapt as women of God, but we must also adapt as helpers. The term "complementary" is crucial to this knowledge as well. It has to be complementary for him. However, being a Helpmeet is not always easy. It involves doing whatever is necessary to complement him. You are not a helper in a way that prioritizes your comfort or insists that you'll do only what you think you should do. No, when God created, He stated, "I'm going to make a helper for him." Therefore, you must understand that you were created for your Husband. Now, that might evoke certain feelings, but you must move beyond that and know you were created for him. Knowing this, you must realize you don't have the right to hold back or withhold because whatever God said was good for him defines who you are.

God showed me I needed to understand that when He talks to me, it is to enable me to assist my Husband and complement him. God provides us as Helpmeets with instructions so we can be well-suited to our Husbands. By doing so, we will do a better job of pleasing God because when He created us, it was to make us helpers for men. The AMP version of Genesis 2:18 contains a word I believe is important for us to examine. It states, "Now the Lord God said, 'It is not good (beneficial) for the man to be alone; I will make him a helper [one who balances him—a counterpart who is] suitable and complementary for him.'" This indicates to me that we were brought into existence to bring balance to our Husbands, to serve as their counterparts, and to be suitable and complementary to them. It has to be advantageous for our Husbands. If you begin to scrutinize the words that come out of your mouth, do they benefit your Husband? Do they balance him? If you're not married, are you benefiting someone? Are you bringing balance to someone? Ask yourself what you are contributing to the equation to be beneficial, suitable, complementary, to be a counterpart, to balance, and to assist. It must be beneficial. God said it.

When we're looking at men, pointing fingers, and asking where all the good men are, we must understand that the good men are indeed out there, but they need not be alone. They don't need to be with just anybody; however, they need the women who are their counterparts and balance them. Sometimes, a man finds that person, but she doesn't realize she's supposed to be his counterpart to adapt and be complementary, resulting in the two remaining in a state of limbo. If a woman doesn't know how to be a Helpmeet, then when the man finds her, he won't receive what he needs. When I didn't know how to be suitable and adaptable, God wasn't blaming me, but He made it clear that I was not suitable for my Husband. I was suitable for the world, the workplace, and the culture, but not for my Husband. The Lord showed me that if I were suitable for him, I would assess his deficits and balance him out. I would consider what he needs and provide it. I would examine what's necessary and adapt to it. This shift changed everything. Until we understand this role, we'll probably continue to see many men in need of help. So, let's now examine a couple more scriptures in this same portion that we are currently studying together.

"And the Lord God caused a deep sleep to fall upon Adam; and while he slept, He took one of his ribs or a part of his side and closed up the [place with] flesh" (Genesis 2:21 AMPC).

"And the rib or part of his side which the Lord God had taken from the man He built up and made into a woman, and He brought her to the man" (Genesis 2:22 AMPC).

Think about these scriptures. God created man and then decided that he needed a Helpmeet. Therefore, He took something from inside the man, built it up, made a woman, and then brought her to the man. You must understand that you are a presentation. You are a gift. This is incredibly important because we don't have the right to withhold from a man, something that God provided for him as his own—something God presented to him as a gift. When we retreat because we dislike something he does or says, or because we are unaware of satan's tactics, we are essentially taking away something that God offered to the man, retracting it from him.

We must comprehend that we were formed and constructed as beings that would need to be brought back to the man and presented to him, so he has the assistance he requires. Understanding this "Helpmeet" role and beginning to perceive ourselves through these verses (Genesis 2:21-22) shifts our mindsets. It transforms our marriage. It transforms our ministry. This is the very purpose for which we were created and what we were intended for. What is our ministry?

God has called us to perform various tasks, but the role of the Helpmeet is what we were created and designed for on the earth. We were initially made to be built up and crafted to provide good help and support. Ministry is who we were created to be to carry out the work of the Lord. I am not saying this is your only ministry or your sole role, but ministry involves doing what God has created you to do. If you skip this part and say you're only a worshiper, or only an apostolic teacher, or only an apostle, prophet, or evangelist, you must remember your primary ministry is to fulfill what God created you to do. As Helpmeets, we have been commissioned to help. We must seek what the Bible is truly saying so we can shift our mindsets according to a biblical foundation.

Consider yourself specifically created for this role. Take a moment and think about that. The reason for your existence, as well as Eve's existence, originated from a thought of God. Not because of her but because of the man. God looked at Adam and said it was not good for him to be alone and determined He would take action; we were the solution. We were the answer. If we lose sight of this, we won't understand why God is instructing us, and we'll miss His guidance. If we lose sight of this, we'll become frustrated with what we're witnessing when things are not working out or proceeding according to our plans. When we observe something out of order, we must remind ourselves that we are the solution. I must choose to remember that I've been the solution from the very beginning. God decided to create a woman to aid the man so that he would not be alone. Therefore, consider yourself as someone who has been specifically created for this role.

CREATED TO HELP

You are created to help. As I mentioned earlier, I want you to understand that this identity of Helpmeet goes beyond marriage. When you study Genesis Chapter 2, you can see that God gave Adam his responsibilities and instructions. Adam and God were spending their own time together. Adam was accomplishing remarkable things, and then a need arose while he was performing the work God gave him to do. Adam was operating within his calling and his true self. He began working, and his efforts exposed a need for assistance. Any work you undertake will reveal a need for help.

When you start a company, you reach a certain point and after a while, you realize you need good help. Anything you build, that starts to grow and function according to its design will require help. Men who are striving to develop into Priests, Prophets, and Kings, and become Kingdom men while trying to find their way to Christ need help. Similarly, when men are attempting to attain deliverance or become good fathers, the work exposes the need for help. A surgeon doesn't need the same type of help as a school teacher. A firefighter doesn't need the same type of help as a nurse. They may not require the same kind of help, but they do need assistance. We must be adaptable and suitable as our specific assignments require that we understand what our men need. If we lose sight of that, we're not good help. We don't want someone doing things that are no help to us—that just gets in the way. It might even be a distraction. In business, this could also lead to losing money unnecessarily.

Doing the work exposed the need within Adam. He began operating and fulfilling what God had created him to do, and then God realized that it wasn't good for him to be alone in his efforts. Adam was performing well. He didn't experience failure initially, requiring God to intervene by setting something in place due to that failure or as a solution to a problem. Instead, God placed the woman beside him so that Adam wouldn't fail. This exemplifies how God operates. While we often tend to react, God is proactive. So, be encouraged as you recall that you were created to provide help.

THE SERPENT OF DECEPTION

Let's continue our reading and see how quickly and suddenly the serpent of deception came onto the scene to disrupt what God had set. "Now the serpent was more subtle and crafty than any living creature of the field which the Lord God had made. And he [Satan] said to the woman, Can it really be that God has said, You shall not eat from every tree of the garden?" (Genesis 3:1 AMPC).

Have you ever considered that the first instance of deception appears immediately in Genesis Chapter 3? After Eve was created to help, satan tempted her. The need for the Helpmeet was identified in Genesis 2:18, and we see satan enter just a few verses later. We observed that God induced a deep sleep upon Adam and then presented Eve as his helper (Genesis 2:21-22). Then in Genesis 2:23, Adam acknowledged that she is bone of his bone and flesh of his flesh. He recognized that because she was taken out of him, she was complementary. She was created to assist him.

As we continue, we read in verse 24 that a man shall leave his father and mother, become united, cleave to his wife, and they shall become one flesh. We see they started as one flesh, but God separated them and then brought them back together. God's objective was for them to return to being one. God was establishing the importance of the man and the woman becoming one flesh. What captures my attention when I study is where it says that a man shall leave his father and mother and become united. The intriguing element here is that this scripture referred to Adam and Eve who did not have a father and mother. This illustrates how significant it was to God's heart that the two unite as one.

As we continue reading, we observe in Genesis 2:25, the final verse of this chapter, that Adam and Eve were naked and unashamed. It was beautiful because God let them know they wouldn't have to be alone. Things were beautiful as God brought a suitable companion for Adam and united the two as one. This concludes Chapter 2. Immediately thereafter, in Genesis 3:1, we see that the serpent came and spoke to the woman. The Bible informs us that the serpent was more subtle and crafty than any living creature of the field that God had created. This is satan, the serpent, the deceiver. So, why did the serpent immediately start speaking to the helper? We must understand that the deceiver knows how crucial the helper is to Adam. It is not a coincidence that this role has been attacked, ignored, and brushed aside. Many attributes of the Helpmeet have been targeted because the deceiver knows the consequences of man being alone.

Eve was created to help, and satan knew that to reach the couple, he needed to target her. The significance of this Helpmeet role must hold meaning for us. It needs to shift our thinking, our minds, and our approach—how we strive and why things are as they are. Genesis 3:1 illustrates the attack on the helper's role because her purpose is to assist. Study this scripture, so the next time you question why you should have to, or when you find the journey challenging and start to murmur and complain, you can recall this scripture. As citizens of the Kingdom, we must step beyond the immediate circumstances and not succumb to deception. We must choose to persevere because God said that it is not good until we are united. It's not good until the man receives his help. It's not good until we operate as one flesh, and this must be our motivation. This motivation is not based on fairytales, wedding dresses, intercourse, or social media likes. It stems from the fact that this was God's design, God's idea.

MARRIAGE IS MINISTRY

Marriage, which serves a specific purpose, was introduced in Genesis Chapter 2 and is attacked in Genesis Chapter 3. Some believe it is for their own pleasure, but I am here to tell you that as a Helpmeet, marriage is not just about pleasing yourself. Often, we want to get married because we desire this or that, and that's great because God grants us the desires of our hearts. However, God established marriage as a solution to a problem. It was a means to complete assignments and accomplish what was needed. God didn't want Adam to miss out on what he needed to do because he was alone and lacked help and companionship. God wanted His assignment through Adam to be fulfilled. This sounds like ministry to me. Marriage is ministry. I want us to take time and reflect on this, as we often overlook and treat it lightly, but it's not

trivial. God created another being due to this purpose, and then satan immediately came to distract her.

When we read Genesis Chapter 3, we see that Eve was talking to the serpent. So the intent may have been good, but the consequences were not based on intent; they were based on God's instructions. God gives us instructions based on what He knows we will face and what He desires from us. God told them they could eat this but not that. How many times has God given us instructions and we've wanted to go the other way? How often has God given us insights and revelations and we've wanted to tweak or adjust them slightly? I want to convey to every Helpmeet that God's instructions are clear. When we start entertaining other thoughts, the tempter begins feeding us lies. He will cunningly suggest that God didn't mean this or that.

I want you to take time and think about who your deceiver is. Write it down. Ask yourself, who is your deceiver? Who is the deceiver using against you? Could it be your culture telling you that you shouldn't submit if you want to be strong and independent? Who is your deceiver and what is it whispering in your ear? Remember Eve was the perfect helper, and the deceiver was trying to convince her that God didn't say what He said. He wanted to persuade her that God was attempting to withhold something from her or keep it hidden. Why would God do that? He is a good God, so He would not. It's easy to look at Eve and wonder why she did what she did, but if we're honest, we can recognize that we sometimes do the same. When God asks you to do something, it's because He has good intentions for you. He knows the challenges you will face and what

He has called you to do. He understands what your partner needs, so He provides you with strategic instructions for your assignments.

This third chapter reminds us that the tempter will say whatever is necessary to divert the help from her assignment. The consequences weren't based on intent. Eve didn't mean to cause any harm, but God's instructions were clear and she did not follow them. Adam trusted Eve, so he ate what she gave him. He knew he had help. He understood that the Helpmeet was created to assist and complement him, and she gave him something so he wouldn't have reason to hesitate. Adam may not have known where the fruit came from. He may not have known that it was from the place God said not to eat from. Did he take it from his helper, assuming she wouldn't do anything outside of helping? It wasn't that they couldn't have any fruit; it was that they couldn't have that specific fruit. So, we don't know if it looked similar to the fruit they could have or not. I am illustrating it in this way because I want us to grasp the concept of this helper role and its significance.

I pray that it starts to open our understanding to things we might engage in that would be analogous to handing our Priest, Prophet, and King a piece of fruit we shouldn't or doing something contrary to what God asked. When Helpmeets receive their instructions and do not follow them, if they are careless or not focused on them, it is similar to Eve giving Adam a piece of fruit from a place he should not partake. So, I want to ask again, what is your deceiver suggesting to you that you have given to your Priest, Prophet, and King, or considered giving him? What are you not providing or doing? All of it is like the fruit Eve gave Adam, and he trusted her. We must follow the instructions God gives us so we don't succumb to the voice of the deceiver.

THINGS TO THINK ABOUT

If we don't change our mindsets and we refuse to ponder this, we will not be consistent because we assume this will come easily. We cannot have the mindset that says, "Just give me the desires of my heart and I will be a Helpmeet long enough to get what I need, and that's it." No, we need to shift our mindsets. Each of us must embrace the role of a helper for ourselves. Here are some things to think about as we change our mindsets concerning this Helpmeet role.

Adam didn't know he needed help. He didn't go to God, asking Him to provide someone because he believed he was falling short or not performing well enough in his assignment. No, God put Adam into a deep sleep because he didn't know he needed help. This is what happened to me. God enlightened me because I was waiting for my Husband to know what he needed—but not even Adam knew what he needed. God did. God had to put Adam in a deep sleep so he wouldn't wrestle with Him, asserting that he didn't require help or he could manage on his own. Sometimes, we question our spouses about their needs, and they might reply that they don't know, leaving us frustrated. But remember, Adam didn't know. Turn to God and seek Him concerning what your Husband needs. The instructions God provides are designed to shield us.

We must silence those deceiving thoughts that tell us our spouses do not want or need our help or won't accept it. The deceiver will offer suggestions that are opposite to the instructions God gave you. If you act on the deceiver's suggestions, you might lose the protection and covering, and consequences will ensue. When you read Genesis Chapter 3 in its entirety, you will see that Adam's response was to eat the fruit Eve gave him because God had given her to him as a helper. Adam understood Eve was meant to assist him because God presented her to him in that way, so he ate the fruit she gave him. They each faced consequences as a result, regardless of whether it was the helper who brought the fruit or both of them participating. Adam ate it and faced consequences as well, leading to complications.

The serpent used Eve against Adam. As Helpmeets, we don't want our Kings to think, "God, you gave her to me, so why is all this happening? If she were operating in her Helpmeet role, aiding me, adapting to my needs, maybe this wouldn't have happened." This is why this role must become a lifestyle. If we start viewing it as a lifestyle, it will change how we perceive the importance of this role. The Helpmeet role is crucial. The deceiver's assignment is to manipulate us against our Husbands, so we must remain vigilant.

I want you to consider the weight of Adam's responsibility on the earth as a result of this. He not only had to manage what he was doing and was responsible for, but he also had to steward his help. He faced consequences because he was the leader. According to Scripture, Eve wasn't present when the instructions were given (Genesis Chapter 17). God provided instructions, but since he was the covering and she didn't do the right thing, he had to assume an additional burden of responsibility. He not only needed to focus on his own tasks but also oversee his helper. Now, you can recognize the weight of your Husband's role (your Priest, Prophet, and King). The magnitude and significance of a Husband's responsibilities are great. Knowing this helps us comprehend why many men are struggling and why a lot of them lack what they need. To initiate healing and realign things according to God's intention, we must understand the weight of a Husband's role.

ARE YOU A HELP OR A HINDRANCE?

We must ask ourselves if we are a help or a hindrance. The deceiver wants us to be "hinder meets," but God wants us to be "Helpmeets." Without understanding the differences in those words, we can become hindrances very quickly. We need to evaluate the areas in which we either are or could be a help or a hindrance to our Husbands. This is part of your homework: examine areas where you feel you are helping and areas where you might be hindering. The goal is to shift your mindset, so begin thinking about aspects of your personal life.

We need to remember that the Husband and wife relationship is unlike any other. It is a one-flesh relationship. So, although principles and concepts such as unconditional love, forgiveness, and speaking things into existence can apply to any relationship, one aspect is different. In this relationship, God expects us to embrace the idea of becoming one flesh. Due to this, there are things that we cannot withhold. There are ways in which we have to think differently. There are things that God is going to ask us to do because He is trying to guide us back to the concept of being one flesh and our ability to complement and restore balance.

RESPECT AND HONOR

In like manner, you married women, be submissive to your own husbands [subordinate yourselves as being secondary to and dependent on them, and adapt yourselves to them], so that even if any do not obey the Word [of God], they may be won over not by discussion but by the [godly] lives of their wives, When they observe the pure and modest way in which you conduct yourselves, together with your reverence [for your husband; you are to feel for him all that reverence includes: to respect, defer to, revere him—to honor, esteem, appreciate, prize, and, in the human sense, to adore him, that is, to admire, praise, be devoted to, deeply love, and enjoy your husband]. (1 Peter 3:1-2 AMPC)

Respect and honor are foundational aspects that we will continuously explore throughout these chapters. This is the mindset we need to adopt. Some of us have found ourselves dependent on circumstances due to our situations and circumstances, but we must keep at the forefront of our minds that God wants us to attain dependence. We need to be capable of adapting to any situation as God leads. Adapt yourself to your Husband. Adapt. We cannot create independence due to circumstances and then resist God's instructions meant to assist us when He gives them. By doing this, we set ourselves up to be out of alignment with God's instructions. This is where the adjustment of our lifestyles needs to occur. We must be clear that God may ask us to alter our way of doing things before we can actually witness their manifestation. Remember, God's thoughts are not our thoughts; His ways are higher than ours. Therefore, we can't merely become dependent on God's thoughts and ways when it's convenient for us. We must be willing to adapt based on His instructions. We can observe in this scripture that God's instructions are meant to help us, even if they may not always make sense to us. The timing may be different, but we cannot allow ourselves to be deceived.

How can we win our Husbands over if we don't follow what God is saying or honor His instructions? The scripture says men will be won over if their wives obey. I often hear this and have responded by saying, "When he does this, then I'll do that." But that is not the right mindset. We need to grasp this understanding quickly to obey and align with God's intentions. Husbands aren't won over by discussions alone; it's the godly lives of their wives that make the difference. Let's revisit the analogy of wisdom. It's not always discussions that win them over; it's godliness and embracing the Helpmeet role. It's the understanding of being a helper, submitting, being subordinate, and dependent that wins them over. We might need to adjust how we do things before we see the changes we desire in our Husbands. It's a plan to win them over. Scripture shows us that when our Husbands observe how we conduct ourselves well, it wins them over. Most men are very visual, so they observe. However, this doesn't mean we wait to be treated in a certain way first. How can they observe something that is not provided? You have to know your role as a Helpmeet because when you understand the Helpmeet role and why you were created, you won't have as many problems operating according to this scripture. You will understand it better and gain deeper revelation. The Holy Spirit will be able to guide you because you will see that God wants you to be in a position to help.

When we conduct ourselves according to Scripture, and we talk about reverence, it encompasses respect, honor, esteem, appreciation, praise, and admiration for our Husbands. It means praising him, being devoted to him, deeply loving him, and enjoying him. Are your Priest, Prophet, and King observing these attributes consistently? God gave us instructions in His Word so that when problems, hurts of the past, or our pain lead us to forget His instructions, we can refer to His Word. We can remember that God created us to help our Husbands. God knows what our helping him will do and what will come out of it. He knows the end of it and is confident in what He is doing. We have to trust the instructions He gives us. We have to obey. God needs our men to be won over and become successful. When we understand the Helpmeet role, we will not question the scriptures about what we are to do because we know why we were created. We must do our part.

Men were created to be honored. The honor they need and desire matches who God created them to be, whether they are apostles, business owners, fathers, or whatever. If a Helpmeet doesn't understand why she was created to help, she won't assist her Husband. In fact, she will hold back and justify her actions. But God knew what the man needed; hence, He clearly identified our role as Helpmeets to honor our Husbands. Women must understand that men will pursue honor in different places if there's a deficit of it at home. Our human nature may cause us to say they need to do something good and then we will honor them, but God's Word tells us men will be won over when we honor them. God needs Helpmeets to trust and see who their Husbands are, who God created them to be and to honor them at that level. We are expected to do what God says.

Let's look at Romans 14:15. It declares, "But if your brother is pained or his feelings hurt, or if he is injured by what you eat, [then] you are no longer walking in love. [You have ceased to be living and conducting yourself by the standard of love toward him.] Do not let what you eat hurt or cause the ruin of one for whom Christ died!" (AMPC). We must understand we have expectations to fulfill as our Kingdom responsibility. We have to answer for the assignment God gave us and created us for. When God speaks to us, He's doing so from His expectations. When we deeply study them, we will gain a better revelation of what He means and why He's saying it. Romans 14:12-13 says, "And so each of us shall give an account of himself [give an answer in reference to judgment] to God. Then let us no longer criticize, blame, and pass judgment on one another, but rather decide and endeavor never to put a stumbling block, obstacle, or hindrance in the way of a brother" (AMPC). We cannot continue to be a hindrance due to our mindsets or lack of understanding. God expects us to be crucified with Christ and be a gift to the body

HELPMEET JOURNAL ENTRY

1. What is God saying to you after reading this chapter?
2. What are some prayer targets you need to add?

~

_____

_____

_____

_____

_____

_____

_____

_____

_____

_____

_____

_____

_____

_____

_____

_____

_____

_____

MARRIAGE

3
THE MINISTRY OF HONOR

s we continue to establish a biblical foundation for the
Helpmeet role, we must understand its biblical nature.
You must realize that this is God's idea because when
things get difficult and the instructions become challenging, that is
what will hold you accountable. Without knowing that this is God's
idea, your flesh may be more inclined to give up when faced with
difficulties. The Bible tells us that faith comes by hearing and
hearing by the Word of God (Romans 10:17), so ensure you are
continually absorbing Scripture concerning this role. Faith is
strengthened every time you encounter something in the Bible that
reinforces it. Accountability is necessary to truly grasp and start to
hear God's heart, not just His voice. We need to hear God's heart for
us as Helpmeets. As we begin to shift and embrace this role
consistently, the enemy will attempt to tempt us and try to dissuade
us from what God has created us to do. Satan may tempt you to
doubt God's love, and these challenges may become so formidable at
times that you might start to think God doesn't want you to walk this
path. Thus, it's crucial to understand His heart regarding the

Helpmeet role. You need to know His heart for you, your family, and as His creation.

This is something you truly have to tap into for yourself. No one else can keep you accountable for this role. When you do this because you know it's God's will and He's asking it of you, then, and only then, will you have enough strength to genuinely embrace this role. The victim mentality is tempting, and if you don't have God's Word in your spirit—meaning you're talking about it, reading it, studying it, and memorizing it—it can create an opening for the enemy or vulnerability to disobedience and rebellion. It makes you susceptible to disobedience and rebellion because the victim mentality can convince you that certain circumstances give you the right to act outside of what God has asked you to do. The Bible states that rebellion is as sinful as witchcraft (1 Samuel 15:23). Once you know that something is God's will and you decide not to follow it, you expose yourself to witchcraft-like rebellion. We don't want to open ourselves to disobedience or rebellion. We strive to become strong enough to understand God's heart and remain steadfast in what He is asking us to do, regardless of where we are in the process.

In this chapter, we will heavily focus on honor, which is something we have to practice because we can assume that we are doing something so well when in reality, we are not. I used to think that I was the greatest wife on the face of the earth. I was confident that I was at least on the top tier—whatever the tier is. I just knew I was at the top because I was doing things well. But God showed me that when it came to the Helpmeet role, I was not. In fact, I was at the bottom tier. Being a good wife is important, but it isn't enough. Honor will change the trajectory of your marriage. Therefore, you must sanctify your life and desire to worship, pray, and fast because you want to be close to God, not just because you need an answer to a problem.

This is how God helped me understand and evaluate myself and how I remain accountable. God challenged me to think about how I would respond if everything was perfect and exactly the way I wanted it in my marriage, money, and every area of my life—would I still fast? Would I pray continually? Would I worship? That is how we can determine whether or not we are truly seeking Him because we want to connect with Him, not just because we are in need in some area.

God fills our cups when we stay in His presence, preventing us from becoming depleted when challenges arise or when we have to give to others. In His presence, we experience an overflow of faith and worship. This overflow occurs as we constantly listen to Him. Additionally, we overflow with goodness and mercy when we are already at His feet. When God requests something for our King, we can readily comply without hesitation; our cups are full. A sanctified wife can also sanctify her Husband. Therefore, when your cup is full because you're continually in God's presence, you will have and carry what your Husband needs. So, sanctification and honor are huge to this Helpmeet role.

To remain in a place of sanctification and honor, you need to ask yourself who is the boss in your mind, house, and heart. Have you checked your tone of voice in response to your King's requests? Can you stop yourself from saying or doing something that you should not? This is a crucial strategy that will help you succeed in this role.

If you can tell when you are out of sorts, being inappropriate, or not honoring and respecting, are you able to stop yourself? Or does it feel so good on your tongue that you cannot restrain it? At the beginning of this journey, I would hear the Holy Spirit tell me not to say or do something at that moment, and with no discipline in that area, things would come out of my mouth, and I would totally ignore the Holy Spirit.

So, as a Helpmeet, let's work on stopping ourselves from doing or saying something that does not reflect honor for God and our King. Can we stop in the middle, correct, or apologize because we know we are outside of God's will, and He is not pleased? If the person doesn't want to hear your apology, then apologize to God and stop doing what hinders you. It's not easy all the time, but ask yourself: who is the boss in my life? Catch yourself, shift, and you will start winning.

I want you to take a moment and ask yourself who comes first in your relationship. If you have kids, it can be challenging to prioritize your King before them. Those who aren't married but already have children should pray, fast, and decree immediately in preparation for putting their Kings first. It is hard to do, but it is biblical. If you can't put your King above your kids in terms of respect, honor, and authority, then you might not be ready for marriage. It's crucial to ready your heart for this concept. And for those already married, who may just be learning this, you'll need to reflect. Your Husband, your King, should come first. If you were to ask your King, would he agree that he's the priority? This is challenging because it's not just about what you think, but also whether he feels he is the top priority. Sometimes we might assume he is unequivocally first, but he might hold a different view. So, pay attention to your actions and responses, allowing your sense of honor to make a leap. I'm not saying your Husband is always right, but I want to emphasize that he needs to hold the primary place in your mindset; otherwise, you might miss opportunities to show honor.

As we continue, let's look at some strategies that will help us to be Helpmeets Suitable who honor God and our Kings.

MY KING'S REQUESTS

As you listen to your King, you will hear him making requests often. I frequently hear that men don't speak or tell us how they feel or even what they want. Many times, if you ask him, you are correct. He may not know how to articulate his feelings; however, when he speaks, he is telling you what he wants. When he shares, he expresses his dissatisfaction. If you listen, you will hear that requests are being made. An example is when he has to ask you if it's a good time to say something. That should tell you that there have been times when he didn't feel he could speak to you, and now he has to ask if it's a suitable time to talk to you. This indicates that he's hesitating to share things because when he spoke before, he didn't receive the reception he desired. In a situation like this, it's as if he is asking for permission to talk to you, and that is out of order. Let me provide another example. If your Husband responds to you by saying he is not your child or he's not a boy, that statement alone is a sign of what he is feeling. It indicates that even if you don't think you're treating him like a child, something is making him feel you're addressing him that way. This is usually a sign that your tone needs adjustment. There is no condemnation, but we must become aware so we can shift and honor our Kings.

When these situations occur, we want to reach a place where we don't get offended. And if we do get offended, we need to address it. Our Husbands are pointing out where we may have fallen short; this is important for us to acknowledge. If we throw it back at them and claim we didn't do what they indicated, we will shut them down from sharing their needs with us. This could make them believe they are not leaders. They will also start to accept that we won't do certain things, and unfortunately, it often shuts men down because they don't feel heard. This takes time to improve, so I challenge you to learn to listen to the requests your King is making. If you're listening intently and comprehending what he is saying, you will understand what he thinks is necessary for him to feel respected and honored. When you internalize the Word of God in your heart, you will recognize this is your responsibility as a Helpmeet. It's important to create an atmosphere where his requests feel comfortable, welcomed, and celebrated. He needs to know you will listen to him and honor what he is saying. Be quick to apologize and be open about your mistakes because he needs to know that his opinions are important to you.

ROLE PLAY

My Husband used to say, "It doesn't matter what I say to you because you're not going to listen to me anyway." I used to hear him say this all the time because we had created a culture where his requests were muted. It reached the point where he didn't think I would listen to him or do what he said, so he stopped asking. There was a lack of honor because I was not listening to him and I did not allow him to feel respected or honored. Keep all of this in mind as you create your own Honor Vision as mentioned in the previous chapter. This is not meant to bring us down but to hold us accountable and align us with God's order of the Helpmeet role. Our Honor Vision is for correction and improvement because we want to align with God's will, not just to get our Husbands to do certain things or to fix our marriage, although that's a manifestation of it.

Role-playing is a significant strategy, and once you engage in it, you will probably want to continue doing so for the rest of your life. This is especially true when you're shifting and changing, as you aim to be better prepared for conversations, opportunities, and open doors.

People often ask me what they should do if they are separated from their spouses and they feel hopeless. My response is to role-play. Most Husbands and wives, especially those who are currently struggling, find themselves trapped in the same arguments repeatedly for years. If you don't break the cycle and do something different, the arguments will remain the same, only in different circumstances. However, through role-playing and reflecting on where things went wrong, you can rewrite the narrative.

When you're feeling frustrated, or angry, or when your emotions are intense, it's difficult to think clearly. It's challenging to hear the Holy Spirit and respond appropriately. So, if you've practiced through role-playing, it will be easier to say the right things in those moments. You'll be accustomed to it, and something different will naturally come out of your mouth.

I will be transparent with my story because I want us to truly understand this. When things were really challenging for my King and me, I could not stand the sight of him. I didn't want to see him at all. When saw him, anger would well up, and you could absolutely see it in my face and hear it in my voice. My responses were sharp and brief. However, when I began to role-play, I started thinking of answers that didn't sound so harsh and were more honorable. This is why I believe role play works. It might not be comfortable for you at first because you may not be at ease with your own voice or having conversations like this. But I encourage you to pretend you are talking to the Holy Spirit. Imagine Jesus is on the other side of the phone or table as you role-play because you wouldn't talk to Him the same way you talk to your Husband. If our Husbands don't see us as honoring them, then they won't ask for help or accept our assistance. This becomes dangerous because then we are out of our role as the helper. When we put ourselves in a position where we can't carry out our assignments; we allow demonic assignments to take root.

STUDY THE WORD OF GOD

Another strategy you must implement for this role is a consistent study of the Word of God. We have to be able to sharpen our ability to hear God, understand the requests of our Kings, and listen to our own voices. We need to study to show ourselves approved. Many of us have grown up with a lazy biblical mindset, so when someone tells us to read our Bible or study Scripture, we often view it as an inconvenience. However, if you can find time to watch a 30-minute television show or scroll through social media for 20-40 minutes, then you can certainly allocate time for studying God's Word. You do have time for studying the Word; you just need to prioritize and desire it. This Helpmeet role requires dedicated study so we remain aligned with God's will. Many people consider going to church as studying the Word but that's not your personal study time. Now, it's imperative to go to church and hear the Word because you will get revelation, but you have to study for yourself.

Studying the Word is necessary, but I see many people struggle because they lack good study habits or don't know how to study the Word. In some cases, they may limit their study to what the pastor has preached. However, I encourage you to open your Bible and engage in personal study. Delve into the Greek and Hebrew meanings of words to enhance your understanding. We must internalize the Word of God to attune ourselves to His voice.

BE STILL

> *"Let be and be still, and know (recognize and understand) that I am God" (Psalm 46:10 AMPC).*

We cannot continue ministry without being still and hearing what God wants us to do. We want to be so still that when He instructs us, although we may not know fully how it is going to look, we will trust that God said it, and we will do it. If everything aligns exactly as you think it should, and nothing challenges you, then most likely God isn't involved. At times, we may declare that something is from God; yet, He doesn't have the opportunity to truly lead or guide it due to our lack of stillness.

I had to truly understand this concept because God repeatedly told me to be still. So, I looked it up, and although I felt I was practicing stillness, God showed me I needed to understand that He is God. I had to realize His ways differ from mine, and His thoughts are higher than my thoughts. This means that I won't always understand what God is asking me to do or what He wants from me. However, by remaining still, I can let go and participate in what He intends to do. I will be able to hear His voice, but I have to actively listen to do so. Take a moment to notice and ask yourself if you are capable of being still because this is not merely an activity to engage in; it's a lifestyle. When you are still, God begins to give you instructions that you would have never considered. God won't always confirm things beforehand. Many times, He confirms them afterward. However, if we've never followed through with what God has asked us to do or heard His instructions, we miss out on these moments.

HONOR

The Greek word for honor is *timē*, and its Greek definition is: "A valuing by which the price is fixed, either of the price itself or of the price paid or received." This means that it's fixed. However, for us as Helpmeets, we want to focus on the next definition: "Honor which belongs or is shown to one; the honor which one has by reason of rank and state of office which he holds" (Thayer's Greek Lexicon, 2011).

The significance of this second definition is very important because it pertains to the office which a person holds. We give honor because of the rank that someone holds, not necessarily the rank that someone operates in. The honor is the office the person holds or has been given. Biblically, in this role as a Helpmeet, we have to understand the office that God has put our Kings in. This is what will make it a lifestyle. It is an office they possess; even if they are not operating in it yet, it is still theirs.

Our culture often dictates that honor must be earned through actions, but this perspective contradicts the role as defined by God. Honor belongs to our Husbands. When you marry your Husband— your Priest, Prophet, and King—you must know that he holds the position of honor as the head. That position is given to him by God, whether you think he is doing a good job of it or not. Whether he is consistent in it or not does not change his position. Accepting this will set you free from questioning whether he deserves certain things or not. You must internalize this understanding to overcome the difficulties and struggles that may arise.

Whether you're preparing for marriage or waiting for your King to find you, you need to ask yourself if you can extend honor before witnessing honorable behavior. This position, the state of the office, the rank that God has given your Husband, is the law. You honor the position because it's God's Word. It's what God says, so we need to honor our Kings because they hold a position that is of God. Once you grasp this understanding, you can begin to operate in the Helpmeet role. When you pray, you will have authority because you're operating in honor. When God asks something of you, you can declare yourself sanctified, and you can now hear God's voice because you're not angry or sinning against His Word, which would open you up to rebellion and witchcraft.

We must receive this revelation. This is my assignment from the Lord: to teach you. Therefore, I pray you will grasp it in your mind and spirit and allow it to transform your way of thinking. If we don't keep hearing this message consistently and discussing it while also storing it in our hearts, we will miss out. Opening ourselves up to disobedience will not only hinder our prayers concerning our marriage, but it will also position us in a place of disobedience. Walking in disobedience will impede your marriage or your marriage preparation.

Some Kings haven't yet found their Helpmeets because their Helpmeets don't understand this yet. The King that God has for you can't afford to have a helper who is off her assignment because he may be dealing with certain issues, and God doesn't want the situation to worsen. Therefore, you need to be in the proper position.

For some of us who are already married, satan is having a field day because we are in disobedience and not operating in honor toward our Husbands. It isn't that we can't understand it because God didn't ask us to evaluate His Word for Him or to decide if we like what He said. This is part of our problem at times; we place ourselves equal to God when we attempt to negotiate what His Word says or if we want to follow it or not. We won't always understand it, but we are not God, so we have to trust His instructions and His Word.

Honor the position of your Husband and you will grow. You will even start to heal. You might need to shift your mindset, instead of attempting to give honor to him, especially when dealing with hurt, dysfunction, or frustration. This can be challenging, but if you shift your mindset and realize that you honor the position because it is

God's will and God's Word, then you can navigate this much more easily. You desire to be in the will of God and honor His precepts.

Let's look at Romans 13:7, "Render to all men their dues. [Pay] taxes to whom taxes are due, revenue to whom revenue is due, respect to whom respect is due, and honor to whom honor is due" (AMPC). We have often misunderstood this to say that when our Husbands show honor, then we will give honor. We have based our actions upon how they act, but the Bible says to give honor to whom honor is due. I am telling you, through the Word of God, that honor is due because the position your King holds is deserving of honor. It is due to him as Your King and Husband as he is in the position of the head. The King doesn't have to operate as the head to be treated as the head.

Now, is it more challenging to honor someone who is not walking honorably? Absolutely. But it is biblical to honor the position since honor is due to the position as the head and covering. We are in God's will when we honor based on the position, not based on our eyes seeing something that is honorable. If you wait and only give honor when you see something that is honorable, it means the moment the person missteps, there goes your honor. In doing so, you have elevated the situation to the status of an idol because the situation and emotion have become more significant than God's Word.

I hear a lot of women say, "I don't want to make him an idol," but this is not making him an idol; it is obeying God's Word. If I am driven by my emotions and not honoring my Husband, then I've made my emotions the idol, not his behavior. If we know God's Word and we don't do what He says, that is on us, and we can't blame it on anybody else.

Have you ever heard someone say confidently, or maybe you have said it yourself, "God told me this" or "God did this," but the minute it gets challenging, all of a sudden, the person says, "Well, I'm not sure if it was God"? How can we be sure it's God when doors are opening—God brings the Husband; you're dating and things are going well; you got the promotion, or favor is coming, but when the man says or does something challenging, we are not sure it's God? Don't open yourself for the enemy to move by getting out of God's will. This is what satan wants for the Helpmeet. The more we align ourselves with God's will, read His Word, and study to show ourselves approved, the more we hear His voice because we are closer to Him. However, in the same way, the further we are from God's will and reading His Word, the harder it is to hear Him.

When we are out of alignment, we might start doing good things because they seem right, but they may not even be from God. If this is the created role for us, as Helpmeets, and we step outside of it, we are halting God's progress and plan, and then we will wonder why we don't hear from Him. If you find yourself in this place, get back in line, and you will start to hear God's voice. There may be things we hear from God that are difficult and challenging for us, but at least when we are in God's will, we can ask Him for the strength, revelation, and strategy to do what He is requesting. We can ask Him for healing in order to do what He is asking us to do. The more we align with God, the better we become at being honorable.

GOD'S PERFECT WILL

We desire God's perfect will for ourselves, our children, our ministry, and all areas of our lives. The God we serve will never ask us to do something that does not ultimately lead to His perfect will. That is His goal—to bring His children into His perfect will.

However, for some of us, our ancestors have fallen out of alignment, or our decisions have led us astray, so God has to guide us back in line with His perfect will. That means there are some back roads that we may have to get on to reroute. God's perfect will is for us to do what's necessary to get back on track with Him. We must ask ourselves if we are actively pursuing God's perfect will for our lives. This is incredibly important because if we are already in His perfect will and we understand His desire outlined in Genesis for the role of a helper, then we must intentionally strive to follow that perfect will.

"Do not be conformed to this world (this age),
[fashioned after and adapted to its external,
superficial customs], but be transformed
(changed) by the [entire] renewal of your mind
[by its new ideals and its new attitude], so that
you may prove [for yourselves] what is the good
and acceptable and perfect will of God, even the
thing which is good and acceptable and perfect
[in His sight for you]" (Romans 12:2 AMPC).

We must not adapt to the external and superficial customs of this age or world because, as those who walk with God, the world is not what we model ourselves upon. Instead, we fashion ourselves after God's Word, His will, and His requests—not after things that are external and superficial. These are the things we see and the things we are accustomed to. We cannot be so fixated on the world that it begins to sway us more than God's Word does. We must be the ones who are transformed by the renewing of our minds.

We don't just want a mere renewal of the mind, a little bit here and a little bit there—absolutely not! We decree a complete renewal. God expects us to experience an entire renewal of our minds, and that tells me our minds need extensive rejuvenation. This process must be continuous. If we go on autopilot, we're setting ourselves up to fall short, and that's how religious notions take hold so quickly; we aren't consistently renewing our minds. If we default to what we've always done, before we know it, the customs of this world will resurface within us. That's what we'll see and what surrounds us. It's what we're accustomed to and what we hear, so we have to transform because we need an entire renewal of our minds. We need new ideals and attitudes. No one else can do this for us because the moment challenges arise or we get hurt, we will return to our old ways. When something comes along that looks or sounds better, we will think that thing is superior.

You have to prove to yourself that this is a Helpmeet role and it is biblical so you will follow it. You must learn how to honor to the point where honor is due. You have to convince yourself that this is God's Word, and you are committed to following it. Ask God what His good, acceptable, and perfect will is. When our minds start to focus on natural things, we need to readjust and remind ourselves of what God said. Therefore, His Word must be hidden in our hearts to strive for God's perfect will. Our entire minds need renewal, which is why I emphasize the mindset so strongly as a Helpmeet. We are striving for God's perfect will, desiring His blessings, favor, healing, and everything connected to it. However, at times, we struggle with renewing our minds. We must reach a point where we see goodness from God's perspective, seeking what aligns with His sight. We need to immerse ourselves in the Word of God to cultivate a hunger and thirst for it; that's the only way we can effectively operate in this role. The renewal of our minds is the sole means to undo what we've absorbed from the world.

There are seasons when I discover my Husband needs an entirely different Helpmeet, and I must turn to God and ask Him how to approach it and what is needed of me. God will provide me with insight, information, and revelation. He will guide me in how to shift and adjust. He will reveal to me that I might need to stop doing this and start doing that. He will unveil things my Husband no longer requires and what he needs now. God will expose to me what the devil is planning for my Husband, and it's all new and different, depending on the season. So, if I weren't already in the habit of seeking God and His Word, I would have assumed I had everything figured out regarding my Husband's needs. I would have continued doing what I was doing because I got good results. God had to show me that if I don't keep coming to Him, then I won't know what's going on. Therefore, I am here to tell you that if you believe you have it all together, figured out, and don't need to learn anything more, then you're already one step behind. This is why the Helpmeet role strengthens your relationship with God; it leads you to rely on Him, not just on what you think, feel, or want. By staying close to God, you will depend on what He wants, thinks, and feels for His perfect will concerning you and your Husband. This is something we must desire because we love and serve God. This is something we have to desire because He is our Lord, and we can't keep calling Him Lord if He can't guide us.

HEALING, FAITH, AND BELIEF

Many people struggle because they are not frequently in God's Word or His presence. People want to assume the role without putting in the necessary work; however, the Bible tells us that faith without works is dead (James 2:17). Why is it dead? Because without the work involved, the faith fizzles out—it vanishes. Healing, strength, and the ability to believe in what God has said, even if it hasn't manifested yet, are all achieved through studying God's Word. Many people lack study habits, so if you find this applies to you, you need to make adjustments. While many people will study business or learn how to make more money or raise their children, they tend to overlook studying the Helpmeet role and what God's Word says about it. Are you consistently studying day in and day out? I encourage you to ask yourself this honestly and adjust accordingly. How can we operate effectively in a role we haven't studied for? We wouldn't consult doctors who are not continuing their education in their field and staying updated on the latest techniques and medicines. How can we excel in this role without dedicating time to the One who created it? This is particularly true when many of us have never witnessed it being properly demonstrated. Many of us have seen it executed incorrectly, and we need to unlearn and correct those misconceptions. We cannot adequately perform and fulfill a role that God specifically created us for if we do not study it.

So, when we find ourselves wondering why we're struggling with this Helpmeet role or questioning whether it should be this challenging, it's often because we are not dedicating time to studying. Sometimes, we say if it's from God, it shouldn't be this hard. However, where in the Bible does it tell us that if something isn't easy, from the perspective of requiring no effort, it isn't from God? It's crucial to realize that something can be difficult and still be aligned with God's will, bringing about the peace that surpasses all understanding, even in the face of difficulty. Many people believe they shouldn't have to work this hard, but why would we think that when the Bible clearly tells us that faith without works is dead? I require faith in this Helpmeet role. I need faith to be married. I need faith to be a good mother. I need faith to be a Kingdom citizen, and faith without corresponding actions is lifeless. Some of us might be experiencing this dormant faith within our marriages because we're not putting in the necessary effort. Thus, we aren't experiencing healing since we haven't studied God's Word concerning this role. It's crucial to realize that the effort is worth it. We must understand that we were created with a natural desire to study God's Word and to internalize His teachings.

People are sometimes taken aback when they hear they need to study the Word of God and train for this Helpmeet role. We seek training for anything we aren't familiar with, so why would this be any different? If we don't know it, we have to train for it, study it, and look it up. We have to read. The more I studied the Helpmeet role, the more I healed because I understood what God was saying and why He was saying it. I comprehended the reasons behind His instructions. When I realized that God was endeavoring to save my Husband's soul, all of His instructions made sense. I desired to no longer feel hurt, have a better Husband, or simply have him leave me alone—these were my options from my own perspective. However, God's desires were different; He wanted my Husband to be delivered and saved. God wanted him to stay, hear His voice, operate in His will, and answer the call God had for his life. As I grasped the heart of God, I found that in His Word through studying, I began to heal because I wasn't as angry anymore. My faith increased as I started to believe through reading God's Word and exploring stories of people overcoming challenges and experiencing healing. I discovered that God is both a deliverer and a healer, so my faith started growing and my emotional pain lessened.

Our marital relationship itself was actually deteriorating. The behavior was worsening. My Husband would tell you that he was indeed becoming worse, but I had an abundance of peace and faith. I started to decree what the Bible says and not solely focus on how it appeared in the natural. This wouldn't have been the case if I hadn't been reading, studying, and believing God's Word. I couldn't believe that this wounded heart was going to heal unless I continued to study about God as a healer and acknowledged that God wanted to heal me so I could assist my Husband. The more I studied and sought understanding, the more it made sense. I understood that God needed to heal me because He wanted to aid my Husband. Studying God's word counteracts unbelief. However, it was a struggle to reach a point where I desired to study. It was a struggle to delve into Greek and Hebrew for clarification. Despite my heartache while my Husband was heading down his own path and making mistakes, I discovered my strength as I diligently studied God's Word and sought Him. I discovered my healing and purpose. I became more attuned to God's voice because I was truly communing with Him. The most effective way to commune with God is to understand His Word and then engage in a dialogue with Him, allowing moments of quiet stillness to hear Him respond.

This Helpmeet role is much larger than we could ever imagine, and the healing we're looking for is found in studying who God created us to be. God created me to be my Husband's helper, and I was struggling with that, so I had to realize if I was going to align with God's perfect will, I would have to operate, not only within my gifts but also as a helper. I needed to do both because that is who God called me to be. Failing at something God desired from me and what pleased God was not acceptable, and I don't believe you're comfortable with that either. So, continue studying the Word of God and observe how things shift.

HELPMEET JOURNAL ENTRY

1. What is God saying to you after reading this chapter?
2. What are some prayer targets you need to add?

~

_____

_____

_____

_____

_____

_____

_____

_____

_____

_____

_____

_____

_____

_____

_____

_____

_____

_____

_____

_____

4
MINDSET

I n this chapter, we are going to focus on a mindset shift. We have discussed our role within the marriage, our ministry to God, and how to honor our Kings. Whether we are married or not, we can tap into this role to prepare for our Kings. We are striving for God's good, acceptable, and perfect will, so we must renew our minds daily to genuinely function as Helpmeets Suitable. We need to ask ourselves if we are renewing our minds completely or if we are only renewing our minds in relation to things we're comfortable with, have heard before, or make sense to us. A challenge for Helpmeets Suitable is renewing our minds beyond our natural understanding.

> "Do not be conformed to this world (this age),
>   [fashioned after and adapted to its external,
>   superficial customs], but be transformed
>   (changed) by the [entire] renewal of your mind
>   [by its new ideals and its new attitude], so that
>   you may prove [for yourselves] what is the good

and acceptable and perfect will of God, even the
thing which is good and acceptable and perfect
[in His sight for you]" (Romans 12:2 AMPC).

This is our assignment from God, and our desire is to fulfill His perfect will for our lives. We aren't fulfilling this role to prove anything to anyone, and we aren't walking according to our own perspective. God often brings this scripture to my attention as a reminder to shift my thinking to His way of thinking. We frequently approach God with our minds focused on things and our desires. Sometimes, we become so comfortable in our relationship with God as our Father that we fail to grasp He is the Lord of our lives. When we understand that fully, He will often give us instructions, and we'll try to speak to Him through our daughter roles, whereas this Helpmeet role truly is going to push us to where we understand Him as Lord. Our mindsets have to shift when we know He is the Lord over our lives. When God begins to tell us what His perfect will is for us, we have to trust Him and adjust. Achieving a complete mindset renewal requires consistent effort. We must ask the Lord if we are conforming to the world's systems or the desires of the flesh in specific areas of our lives, especially if we intend to operate effectively as Helpmeets Suitable.

IS IT POSSIBLE?

This role will challenge our belief in the Word of God. God expects us to tap into Him supernaturally so that we can operate in it. He's not expecting us to do it alone. This is where you partner with God, and whenever you encounter something that seems impossible, you must quickly pull it down and declare the Word of God. This requires crucifying our flesh. When you realize that the enemy is challenging your belief in the Word of God, your response must be to stand firm in your faith in God's Word.

IS IT SUSTAINABLE?

This role will either enhance or expose our faith. I can relate to starting off well and then stopping when I encounter something contrary to what I want to see or what I asked the Lord for. This Helpmeet role both enhances and exposes our faith and tenacity. You might wonder if this role is sustainable, and the answer is absolutely, but only through God and only through faith. It's only when we understand that we are beings who must relinquish our wills to God's will to operate within it.

As I've been learning about this role, I've found that God created certain situations to draw us back to Him. Over time, what has happened in the body of Christ is that we have removed elements from the Word of God. However, if we are truly operating in this Helpmeet role, we will have to continuously crucify our flesh. Many people don't like that concept, but it's rooted in the Bible. When we read, understand, and study the Word of God, it's an act of faith to move beyond what we can see.

I want you to ask yourself if you can maintain your belief in God's Word without visual evidence of it manifesting in your life. Pause and consider if you can persevere, even when you don't see immediate results. This applies not only to your Helpmeet role but also to your Christian walk and your growth in the Kingdom. Truly, the Helpmeet role provides us with practice for our daily Christian walk. Can you continue to fulfill what God has asked of you with no immediate return?

Many times, we impose timeframes on what God says, and when we don't see His promises materialize within that time, we start to present Him with a playback or a report card, attempting to convince Him that we shouldn't follow through with what we know He has asked us to do. During challenging times, we need to remind ourselves that we may not be able to see God visibly, but we know we are not alone. This is sustainable, but we have to make a shift. God's Word is not meant to harm us; it was intended to mature us and build our relationship with Him. I can't speak for you, but I strongly believe that the Helpmeet role has done that for me as I've aimed to be suitable. I've had to set aside my own desires and will and remind myself that it is God's will that I desire. I've had to let go of what I think I should have, when I think I should have it, and the timeframe it needs to happen, which exposes my faith. Prayerfully, as I continually operate in this role, my faith becomes enhanced. I don't want my faith to be exposed, and for someone to look at it and find it weak. I desire for my faith to progress from one level to another. I want my faith to grow stronger and stronger.

So, when you begin to declare that this is sustainable, it will reveal your level of faith. According to Romans Chapter 12, God has given each of us a measure of faith. We need to tap into Him supernaturally to access it. When challenges arise and satan tries to tempt you to step outside of this role (and it will happen), your faith needs to increase, and you must draw on scriptures to sustain you. It's biblical to ask the Lord to increase your faith. When you come to a point where you want to quit or ease up on the assignment and calling, ask God for an increase in faith.

MATURITY VERSUS LONGEVITY

This role will force a maturity in Christ. Sometimes, we decide that because we have been in church for a long time, have read the Bible for many years, have grown up in the church, or held a title for an extended period, it equates to maturity in Christ. However, when we begin operating consistently in this role, we come to realize that longevity is irrelevant. Maturity is necessary. Longevity does not equal operating in this role. This role requires maturity because it will force you to be more developed in the things of God. It will prompt you to engage with the Word of God in a different way. This role will require you to tap into your relationship with God and dedicate time to Him.

I wasn't consistently tapping into seeking God unless I wanted something. I loved God. I was operating in His Word and even served as a pastor. However, I desired and spent time with God to get specific things I wanted. Maturity is when I'm consistently tapping into God, speaking to Him, and creating a lifestyle of going back to Him for instructions. It involves communicating with Him and establishing a routine of returning to God for guidance. It necessitates continuously seeking God for information and direction. I believe this role is designed to keep us at the forefront of our Christian journey. When maturity kicks in, it prompts you to question whether you truly know God and His Word or if you are simply acting out of habit due to the passage of time.

ONGOING COMMUNICATION

This Helpmeet role requires reliance on the voice of God. I had to learn how to silence the voice of my flesh, which is essentially the voice of a stranger—the voice of the enemy. I needed to cut out the desires of my flesh that resulted from the enemy's temptations. Often, we know exactly what the Holy Spirit has said, but it's difficult, so we might opt to listen to the voice of our flesh. Sometimes, we might prefer to heed what feels good or sounds agreeable to us, but there's no way to truly operate as a Helpmeet while continually listening to the wrong voice. We must maintain consistent communication with God. Much of what is required in this Helpmeet role doesn't make natural sense. The Word of God instructs us to pray for those who mistreat us, a concept that doesn't align with the natural mind. Hence, we need to rely on God. If you're unsure whether you're hearing the voice of God, you must read the Word because the more scriptures you know, the better you'll recognize when God is speaking. To follow God's ways, we must adhere to His instructions, which are found in His Word and through His voice. I encourage you to spend time with God daily. Ask yourself if you are making time for God.

MAKING TIME WITH GOD

> "Look carefully then how you walk! Live
> purposefully and worthily and accurately, not as
> the unwise and witless, but as wise (sensible,
> intelligent people), making the very most of the
> time [buying up each opportunity], because the
> days are evil. Therefore do not be vague and
> thoughtless and foolish, but understanding and
> firmly grasping what the will of the Lord is"
> (Ephesians 5:15-17 AMPC).

We must decide to be sensible, intelligent, and wise people. We must become those who make time for God and devotion. It's necessary to spend time simply soaking in the presence of God. During our time with Him, we must create opportunities to understand what is necessary to live purposeful, worthy, and accurate lives that align with His perfect will. We don't want to be unwise and live a life based on our interpretations of what God is saying or telling us.

If you quiet yourself with the Lord and inquire of Him often, you'd be surprised at what God will ask of you and reveal to you. Sometimes, when I seek and inquire of God, what He says doesn't match what I am accomplishing or what I think His Word means in a particular area. As I begin reading and studying, He provides more insight. When I start talking to God, He reveals what He wants and needs. When I become quiet before Him, I gain a different revelation because His ways are not my ways, and His thoughts are not my thoughts. We must spend quality time taking opportunities to listen to God. We have to be purposeful and accurate with our time; otherwise, we might do what seems right but not necessarily what is truly beneficial.

We can usually distinguish between good and evil because we have a conscience, and most of us have been brought up to be aware of good and bad. However, in this Helpmeet role, we have to be able to discern between good and God. Just because something is good doesn't mean it's the right thing for us at that moment. It may not be precisely what God wants for you at that time. So, as you spend time with God, you will become more familiar with His voice. Make time for God. When God says something to you and you're not sure how you're supposed to move forward with what He said, you need to spend more time with Him and allow Him to guide you further while restraining your flesh's desire to engage in other activities because you think you don't have time to sit with God.

You have to spend time fasting and worshiping. Get resources and books to fulfill what God has spoken to you. Whenever I told God I was too busy, He would challenge me and ask what I was too busy for. That scared me because I realized I was consistently telling Him I didn't have time to do what He wanted from me. If God is asking me to do something, then I have to trust that there is a way to accomplish it through Him. The Lord instructed me to evaluate my days differently. He allowed me to assess some of the good things I was doing, enjoyed, and was skilled at, as well as tasks I had been doing for a long time that people appreciated. But I had to reevaluate them because God was asking me to give up some of them.

God began to show me that this Helpmeet role is a priority. He worked it out supernaturally, but He needed me to relinquish my flesh first. I had to let go of my will for His will, but it required time. God's Word demands that we make some shifts, and it takes time in the beginning because it's almost foreign to us. Think of it as a new workout; our muscles aren't ready for it right away, so we often stop because we don't like the way it feels. We halt because it's difficult, but I'm encouraging you that as you move forward, you will start to feel more comfortable. I won't say it will be easy, but you will become more adaptable.

Your vocabulary will change; your mindset will change, and your habits will change. I want to encourage you while you are studying this Helpmeet role not to allow the enemy to overwhelm you into thinking it will always be this challenging. It will challenge you because that's what God's Word does, but it will become normal for you.

I also want to encourage unmarried women to truly understand this, so that it won't feel so foreign to them once they get married. When we grasp this, we will operate in it in front of our daughters. They will start to learn from it, and it will make sense to them as they grow older. They will observe us forgiving and living out the Word. Our daughters will witness us spending time with the Lord and being women of devotion. This is training up our children in the way they should go. They will watch us, and it will shape their understanding of relationships and faith. We need our children to witness this consistently. We must live the Word.

JOURNAL DISCOVERY

I encourage you to put together a Helpmeet journal because this is a journey, and your own writings will be a source of self-encouragement. Date your journal entries, so you can look back at what you wrote and see how far you have grown. God inspired me to highlight Ecclesiastes 3:11 as we continue in this study.

> *"He has made everything beautiful in its time. He also has planted eternity in men's hearts and minds [a divinely implanted sense of a purpose working through the ages which nothing under the sun but God alone can satisfy], yet so that men cannot find out what God has done from the beginning to the end"* (Ecclesiastes 3:11 AMPC).

God makes everything beautiful, but time is attached to it. Your purpose and destiny take time, so I am encouraging you to continue journaling. You don't have to do it every night, but periodically write down what the Lord is speaking to you and what's on your heart as you spend time with Him. Listen to God's instructions and start to map out what He is revealing to you. Remember it takes time, and God makes everything beautiful in its time. There is the *kairos* time of God for things to shift. I believe this is the greatest time in the body of Christ because God is getting ready to do some things swiftly. If we are not ready, we may miss them. We might see someone gaining things we were praying for but weren't prepared to receive. We'll observe individuals moving quickly in their purpose, destinies, marriages, families, and finances, and we'll wonder what happened. But remember God's timing is up to Him.

We need to be deeply rooted and grounded in God's purpose and divine plan, realizing that all things work together for our good. This is where we have to trust and believe in Him. We must decree that we will see the benefits in our children, marriages, purpose, destinies, and ministries. Here, we must trust God with our whole hearts and not lean on our own understanding. It might not be something we fully understand, but we still have to trust Him and have faith. We need to align our ways with God's perfect will. He knows the end from the beginning. He knows the plan and purpose He has for us and since He knows the plan, He also knows the route to His plan. His plan for each of us is good and not evil. He will not lead us in the wrong direction.

BLOCK DISTRACTIONS

I want you to seek God and take a look at who is a potential distraction in your life. Sometimes, you'll be surprised by what you discover. Once you identify who is distracting you, create a plan to deal with them in a loving but swift manner.

We need to realize that God's expectation is for us to leave and cleave, especially when we are not married and are eager to hurry up and get married. We must be prepared to leave and cleave. When things are going smoothly, it's easy to leave and cleave, but when challenges arise—and they will—the process of cleaving is tested.

During such times, we may be tempted to go back and make statements we shouldn't, or realign ourselves with old lifestyles, places, or relationships. Be mindful of this and ask yourself again who is a potential distraction?

First, create your own list. You may be able to easily identify a relationship that is a distraction from your Helpmeet role. We cannot prioritize any person above our relationship with our King. If there's anything that God presents to you that you wouldn't be willing or able to let go of if He asked you to, for the sake of your King, you are out of order.

Go back to Genesis Chapter 3, just after God created the Helpmeet. God didn't want Adam to be alone, so He created a helper for him. He immediately instructed them to forsake their mother and father and to leave and cleave. This principle is present in Scripture, serving as a reminder that we must forsake everything else, and yes, that includes children.

There were times when God instructed me not to do certain things for my children in order to make time for my King. I underwent multiple deliverance sessions concerning actions that God deemed a priority for my King's deliverance. I had to set aside some activities I wanted to do for my kids that were beneficial. As a result, I engaged in debates with the Lord about it.

As Helpmeets, if we zero in on the godly instructions to leave and cleave, we will experience growth. Often, we approach God, attempting to justify ourselves or explaining why we don't want to do what He has directed us to do. We avoid asking God certain questions and instead begin to list the reasons we have for not following Him.

The enemy easily places distractions in our path that seem right and good. One of the most challenging aspects of my journey was when my family started labeling me as a bad mother. This was difficult because I recognized that while I might not have been a good Helpmeet, I knew I was a good mom. At that time, God asked me whether I was more concerned with their opinion or His. It took time for me to realize I had been prioritizing their perception of me over God's perception of me, and I needed to grow.

For many of us to truly operate as Kingdom citizens, women of God, Helpmeets, and spiritual warriors, we must align ourselves with the Word, rather than with what's comfortable or culturally accepted. This is why one of our core scriptures is Romans Chapter 12. We cannot conform to this world; we need to be transformed by the renewing of our minds. So, as you work through this area in your life, start by asking yourself who you believe is a potential distraction. Then, spend time asking God who He perceives as a potential distraction in your life. Afterward, compare your lists and formulate a solid plan. At times, God may reveal certain individuals, and this can be challenging, especially if it's someone who has been your best friend for your entire life. They might be leading you in the wrong direction, and God may be guiding you toward a different path.

There were people in my life who weren't bad; they were good and honest, caring and loving. However, I wasn't strong enough to be around them. These weren't people living sinful lifestyles or anything of that sort, but they were engaged in activities outside of the Helpmeet role, and whenever they did those things, I found myself wanting to do the same. I remember feeling frustrated that I couldn't partake in their actions, and I began losing my way due to the distractions. God revealed to me that I needed to sever those relationships. Some of these changes were temporary, while others I have yet to reconcile. God showed me how to gently transition away from certain things and become less available in those relationships. Some of those connections were shifting my Kingdom perspective, pulling me backward.

Once you've identified who is causing distractions and created a plan, it's important to regularly review the plan to ensure you stay aligned. Constantly ask yourself, "What are potential distractions?" First, focus on the "who," and then consider the "what." Sometimes there are addictions, sins, hobbies, places, and activities that could divert our attention from our Helpmeet roles. I held various positions in the community, but God instructed me to let go of some of them. I would resist and remind God that I wanted to continue, that I excelled at those roles, and that they needed me. However, God affirmed that while I was indeed capable and accurate, I needed to realign with His will. I had to fast and pray about some of these distractions. In fact, I'm still fasting and praying about them. There are times I need to go back to God and ask if I can engage in something He had advised me against. He might say I can, but He reminds me that if I want to operate fully in His will, I must obey.

4 IMPORTANT KEYS TO THE KINGDOM HELPMEET ROLE

Studying is the first key that I want to restate because it is vital to your assignment, role, and journey. It is a lifestyle for a Kingdom citizen. To be suitable and adaptable, we must realize that this will require consistent studying, which allows us to remain suitable and adaptable. This isn't just for us as Helpmeets but for women of God altogether. Without reading and studying God's Word, we will not grow in the things of God. We not only have to study God's Word but also ourselves. We must study our finances, health, relationships, and everything concerning our lives. As we study, God will reveal to us how to do things, but we must put in the work because the Bible tells us that faith without works is dead.

The work is studying and learning. Being watchful in intercession and the spirit is a key to staying complementary as a helper. We have to watch as well as pray. We must continually look for things that could distract us and throw us off because every season is not the same. Many people don't realize that part of our assignment is to be watchful enough to know what could get in our way or what could bother us. We have to watch so we can adjust and remain flexible when needed. We not only have to watch for ourselves but also for our kings, our families, and everything associated with our lives. All of us have assignments of intercession and prayer.

Instruction is the third key I want you to remain mindful of as you operate in your role as a godly Helpmeet. God will provide divine instructions in various ways concerning His will for our Husbands. Therefore, we need to realize, as Helpmeets, that God does not want us to go into this journey blindly. When I genuinely asked God what He wanted me to do concerning certain aspects of my life, it was as though He was giving me personal intel and insight into the things I was inquiring about. When I stopped resisting God's instructions, it truly blessed me, as I could then listen intently for His guidance. God may communicate through dreams, visions, insights, and prayer targets regarding the things you inquire about. He may also reveal demonic assignments. Therefore, when God gives us instructions, we must be mindful of them and understand that they are divine. These instructions may not always be things we like or even understand. However, when they are from God, they are divine. It's important, as a key to this role, to recognize that God is going to instruct us, and we must follow what He says fully. Order is important to God; as He takes care of the head, He knows that His daughters will be taken care of. If God can get the head of the family lined up and bowed down before Him, listening and operating in his role, then all the things that the head covers will be accomplished. God's instructions to us often focus on the head because God is a God of order. So, write down what God instructs you, as it can be easy to forget some of the things He has told us, and we can easily deviate from those instructions. The more I operate in this role, the more I realize the necessity of writing down or recording what I am hearing from the Lord.

Order is the final key I want to share with you. As Helpmeets, we are responsible for the atmosphere of the home, so if we understand order, then we will also understand how to shift the atmosphere. We will comprehend how to establish the proper atmosphere for our particular home, our specific gifts and callings, our individual King, and our distinct bloodline. It isn't the same for everyone. Drawing from my experience as a former administrator, I was always focused on people's individual education plans. I was cognizant of the need for differentiated instruction because one child learns or responds a certain way, while another child operates completely differently. I was aware that one parent's needs would differ from another, and one department's needs would also differ from the other. This allowed me to maneuver back and forth, and the order in our home is similar to that. God doesn't give everybody the same instructions. He provides us all with the same framework according to His Word, but He will give you specific instructions on how to maintain order in your particular home.

The Lord guided me to do very specific things in my home. He told me which scents to put in the house, where to place them, and when to turn them on. He also guided me on where to place the television and other similar details. There were instructions about the atmosphere of the home that brought order to the household and the environment. This, in turn, brought order to our relationship and contributed to my Husband's deliverance. Those instructions were key and made a significant difference. If God gives you instructions and you find yourself thinking that you're beyond them or that you shouldn't have to follow all that He is asking, then you might not be fully submitted. This lack of submission can hinder you from fulfilling your role as a Helpmeet Suitable for your Husband and your home. When you can create an atmosphere where your King feels like a King, where he is comfortable and calm, it brings about a change. If there is peace in the household, it extends to the King, making these keys essential for your benefit. Consistency is crucial so that your King can rely on it.

Pause for a moment and ask God about the things He has shown you that you didn't continue doing, or perhaps you didn't do them at all. Write them down as you hear them. They may be small but take this moment to jot them down. This is about being obedient to the Lord's instructions. It might be challenging, so don't rush through it. I understand that this could truly be difficult for those who are separated from their Kings because there was a time when God would ask me to do things in the home, and I didn't even know where my Husband was. In fact, he wouldn't even return my calls at that time. But God asked me whether I was doing these things for him or if I was doing them simply because the Lord said so. It was a challenge, so I had to change my entire way of thinking.

When God asks us to do something, the only reason we should stop is if He gives us the okay to do so. If we're not consistent with God's instructions regarding one thing, He can't provide us instructions for the next. Therefore, we must become accustomed to hearing His still, small voice. Your goal is to start and remain faithful over the little things. During the time God had me setting the atmosphere in my home, my Husband wasn't here yet. However, what God was instilling in me was the establishment of a habit while he was away.

God will ask you to do certain things, especially if you aren't married. If you're unable to follow instructions now, it's unlikely you'll simply wake up one day and do it. We need to work on our obedience and discipline. Our desire is for God to trust us with our partners, so we must be capable of carrying out the tasks He requests of us.

WHAT SETS HELPMEETS APART

The word "sanctified" means to be set apart. It is about being separated for God's use. It means being different, not like the world, and having our mindsets renewed. God makes provision for one spouse to participate in sanctification, and it's rooted in the Bible. The world tells us that it takes two for marriage to become sanctified, but the Bible tells us that a sanctified wife can also sanctify her Husband. Don't allow the enemy to tell you that this isn't from God.

Better communication sets us apart as Helpmeets. Conversations are not avoided between a Husband and wife when unconditional love is consistently felt. Communication is very easy when people consistently feel unconditional love. You don't want to avoid a person who is showing you unconditional love. I am not saying it will always be easy, but God set this thing up so it will work; we just have to put in the effort. If you are in a situation where you're separated, work on being able to show unconditional love yourself. It is not easy to show unconditional love when someone else's attitude, speech, or behavior toward you is contradictory. Our natural minds are trained to treat people the way they treat us, but that's not our goal. That won't make us suitable. Unconditional love takes work. If I'm continually working toward operating in unconditional love, then communication with my King will improve. Many marriages break down because we are unable to cultivate good communication, but if unconditional love is shown by just one person, it will cause the other to soften.

Intimacy also sets us apart as Helpmeets. Honor and respect create an atmosphere for physical and emotional intimacy. As a coach, counselor, and a woman, I understand that sometimes healing is necessary to work on intimacy. However, at times, we prolong our healing because we are hesitant about being intimate. Be intentional about healing so you can overcome it and align biblically with what rightfully belongs to your Husband. Refusing your Husband in areas of intimacy is not in line with the Bible. While this might not be what some want to hear, remember that your body does not solely belong to you; it belongs to your Husband. It's crucial to align yourself so you can be intimate with your Husband.

Intimacy with our spouses should be our desire. There may be times when Kings don't want to be intimate, and I understand that we cannot control people. However, we must work on establishing an atmosphere of honor and respect where our Kings feel they can trust us enough to be intimate. It works both ways. If a Husband does not want to be intimate for whatever reason, take it to God in intercession.

Righteousness sets us apart as Helpmeets. When we operate in righteousness, all things will be added, and prayers will be answered. Since I need all things added to my life, I strive to be righteous. We are called to seek the Kingdom of God and righteousness first, so we need to ask God for help in being righteous. Healthy marriages, families, good health, finances, and aligned Priests, Prophets, and Kings operating in God's will are essential. The enemy deceived me for a long time, tempting me and making me feel entitled to act outside of God's will. We must take the time to seek God's guidance to correct our actions. When we are not in line with God's instructions, satan—the accuser—will continuously bring it against us, hindering our prayers. Therefore, it's imperative to stay in biblical alignment.

We may not always like God's instructions from our human perspective, but aligning with them accelerates our healing process. This, in turn, allows God to open the windows of heaven and pour out blessings upon us. Our prayers are answered, and all things can be added to us. By aligning ourselves with the Bible, satan's influence diminishes. God cannot contradict His Word. I had to learn to adjust my thinking, attitude, and actions to align with Scripture.

SERVICE TO GOD

> "Wives, be subject (be submissive and adapt
> yourselves) to your own husbands as [a service] to
> the Lord" (Ephesians 5:22 AMPC).

We must operate in this role to please God, not because we want to get married, reconcile, or satisfy our families. If we embrace this role to do God's will, be obedient to Him, and hide His Word in our hearts to avoid sinning against Him, then we will have the supernatural strength to carry it out. When we act based on our personal motives, we won't acquire the strength; we might start and stop, and even attempt to dissuade others from pursuing it. Ephesians 5:22 saved me. When God directed me to this scripture, I had to completely change my mindset. I am incredibly thankful that it did, as it provided me with the strength to redirect my focus away from my Husband's behavior and our struggles.

Everything changed for me when I truly grasped the understanding of this scripture. I needed to internalize it, not merely read or write it. This scripture had to be rooted deep within my spirit and I encourage you to memorize it. We operate in submission to our Husbands because we are here to serve our Lord and Savior. This is our purpose as servants of the Lord. I must be submissive and adapt to my Husband, even when it may seem unnecessary or when I'm not inclined to. I must remember that this is my service to the Lord. Although my Husband and family benefit from my obedience to the Lord in this, I don't do it primarily for them, but for God.

We can forget that this is God's will when our emotions are all over the place, and frustration takes hold. Additionally, when we hear people advising things contrary to God's will, and our own desires are stirred, we must keep this scripture in our minds. If you're not submissive and don't adapt, you cease to serve the Lord fully. Your service is to be in submission to your Husband; it's an integral aspect of your service to God. Through this, we demonstrate that God is Lord over our lives, yielding our will to His. The subsequent scripture addresses the Husband's role, but I can't speak for my Husband. When I stand before the Lord, I will answer for whether I've truly served God in this manner. Recognizing that this directive is a part of the Bible and constitutes your service to God can help you overcome the enemy's temptations. I've firmly resolved that nothing and no one will obstruct me from serving the Lord.

We mustn't solely rely on what we perceive or how we feel. This scripture (Ephesians 5:22) empowered me in life's extreme challenges. When I didn't want to please my Husband, I had to remind myself that my ultimate goal was to please God. During those times, my aim wasn't merely about pleasing my Husband, but rather about pleasing God.

In the next chapter, we will delve into the profound significance of the Helpmeet role in our lives. Grasping our genuine identity and purpose is essential for fulfilling God's plan for us. Differentiating between being a Helpmeet and a wife is crucial, as they carry distinct meanings. Our assignment in Titus Chapter 2 guides us to teach and embody appropriate doctrine, reflecting genuine Christian character. Throughout our journey, my Husband and I have gained valuable insights that we now share to assist others. Embracing the Helpmeet role transforms every aspect as it originates from God Himself. Aligning with His will necessitates discipline and discernment. By comprehending God's Word, we empower the healing and growth of our marriages, embracing our call to be both submitted and strong, exemplifying qualities of goodness and kindness.

HELPMEET JOURNAL ENTRY

1. What is God saying to you after reading this chapter?
2. What are some prayer targets you need to add?

～

_____

_____

_____

_____

_____

_____

_____

_____

_____

_____

_____

_____

_____

_____

_____

_____

_____

_____

_____

_____

5

I WISH I KNEW ABOUT BEING A HELPMEET EARLIER

B ut [as for] you, teach what is fitting and becoming to sound (wholesome) doctrine [the character and right living that identify true Christians]. Urge the older men to be temperate, venerable (serious), sensible, self-controlled, and sound in the faith, in the love, and in the steadfastness and patience [of Christ]. Bid the older women similarly to be reverent and devout in their deportment as becomes those engaged in sacred service, not slanderers or slaves to drink. They are to give good counsel and be teachers of what is right and noble, So that they will wisely train the young women to be sane and sober of mind (temperate, disciplined) and to love their husbands and their children, To be self-controlled, chaste, homemakers, good-natured (kindhearted), adapting and subordinating themselves to their husbands, that the word of God may not be exposed to reproach (blasphemed or discredited). (Titus 2:1-5 AMPC)

To comprehend your Helpmeet role, you must know your identity. You need to understand why God created you and who He intended you to become. He designed you to be a Helpmeet, endowing you with gifts and talents. When God observed Adam and acknowledged his solitude, He explicitly stated, "I'm going to make him a helper," but this helper came with a distinct purpose. Among her tasks was her Helpmeet role, but what about her other aspects? What about the endeavors she was uniquely called to pursue? I am deeply appreciative that I have come to discern the contrast between a Helpmeet and a wife, as they are distinct entities. They are crafted differently. A Helpmeet embodies a posture and a standard—a godly responsibility. Being a wife holds significant importance, but it doesn't automatically signify being a helper.

In my studies, I've realized I have a Titus Chapter 2 assignment. I sincerely wish I had possessed the knowledge that I have now. But now that I am enlightened, it's my duty to share. Let's read this passage of Scripture in Titus 2:1, "But as for you, teach what is fitting and becoming to sound wholesome doctrine, the character and right living that identify true Christians" (AMPC). This discusses the ability to teach sound doctrine that is suitable for the moment, the audience, and the context. Certain actions we engage in while evaluating our hearts, as we learn how to be helpers, determine whether we are genuinely Christians. When I began functioning as a Helpmeet, I recognized that I wasn't as strong or spiritually mature as I had assumed. However, as a Titus Chapter 2 woman of God, I must ensure that I'm teaching sound doctrine to accurately identify true Christians.

Now, let's delve further into Titus 2:3, which states, "Bid the older women similarly to be reverent and devout." This means I must adhere to God's assignment. People might wonder why I consistently talk about being a Helpmeet, but it's because I must show reverence for what God has revealed to me. I must remain devoted to God's assignment for my life. The verse continues, "In their deportment as becomes those engaged in sacred service, not slanderers or slaves to drink." When you fulfill what God has called you to do, it's considered a sacred service. You don't dismiss or ignore it. You envelop yourself in it and say, "God, if you created me for this, I will do it well." The verse continues, "They are to give good counsel and be teachers of what is right and noble."

Moving to Titus 2:4, "So that they will wisely train younger women to be sane and sober of mind (temperate, disciplined), and to love their Husbands and their children." Finally, let's examine Titus 2:5, "To be self-controlled, chaste, homemakers, good-natured, kindhearted, adapting, and subordinating themselves to their husbands, so that the Word of God may not be exposed to reproach (blasphemed or discredited)."

As I've been studying this Titus Chapter 2 assignment, something ignited inside of me. I want to take what God has shown me—something I wish I had known earlier in my marriage—to help you and others overcome and gain a more thorough understanding of our Helpmeet role. My goal is to spare you from making the same mistakes I did.

The portion of scripture I'm referring to was written by Paul. When he wrote it, he aimed to establish a godly church by fostering godly character, imparting godly teachings, and raising up godly leaders. This was because when these leaders comprehend something, even if it proves difficult and challenges human nature, they show reverence to the Lord's assignment by teaching it.

Throughout my journey of learning and teaching the Helpmeet role, there were many instances where people would look at me, speak ill of me, and grow frustrated with me. This was because the concept challenged their human nature (carnal man). However, once you truly grasp your assignment, it becomes a reverent calling to operate within it.

As a leader, it would be irreverent of me not to share and teach you about the mistakes I made in my marriage so that you can learn from them. Does that mean my Husband never made mistakes? Absolutely not. When you hear our testimony and the experiences we went through, you'll understand that our marriage faced some horrifying situations. Some of the worst things imaginable happened. Yet, I am here to convey that understanding God's assignment as a Helpmeet has the power to shift everything.

When I finally understood what a Helpmeet meant to God, not just to my Husband, it became important to me because I realized it was God's idea. It needed to be something that I focused my mind on. I grew up in church, so I understood the difference between good and evil. However, as I began to mature, I also had to discern the difference between good and God. You must comprehend that some actions that you can take aren't necessarily bad things, but they might not be appropriate at that specific time. They don't align with your Helpmeet role. They might not be suitable for your particular situation or circumstances. There is a distinction between what is considered good and what is aligned with God's intentions.

So, as I operate in this Titus Chapter 2 assignment, it is my reverent and sacred duty to educate more individuals about how to be a Helpmeet that is appropriate and fitting. I understand that sometimes it's challenging and painful, but it's my sacred responsibility to offer sound guidance, not just the advice that someone wants to hear. My guidance will be based on the Word of God.

The portion of scripture that we just read instructs us to carry out these actions to effectively train young women, enabling them to possess sound and sober minds (being temperate and disciplined). There needs to be more discipline both in marriage and within the body of Christ. The body of Christ must be capable of reading Scripture and making decisions based on it. As you undergo training to become a Helpmeet, you will learn to cultivate discipline as God will lead you to undertake tasks you've never encountered before. You will need to dig deep, and let me tell you, I certainly had to do so. I can't speak for you, but I had to dig and continue digging deep into the Word of God. That's why I often say that I wish I knew then what I know now. I was unaware of spiritual warfare. I didn't know I could break down strongholds. I wasn't aware that I could cancel generational patterns. I didn't know I could decree and declare as I do now. I didn't possess the understanding back then that I have now. So, in this Titus Chapter 2 assignment, I had to learn how to bring my body under subjection and teach it to comply.

Understanding God's Word became incredibly important for the healing of my marriage. God performed new things, and now I can function within the realm of His calling for me. I desire to share all that He has revealed to me. During this season, God is urging me to teach women that they can be both submitted and strong according to His ways, not the ways of the world. God's instructions might appear unreasonable to some people in your life, but I encourage you to embrace discipline, self-control, goodwill, kindness, and all these attributes that align with God's ways.

To be a Helpmeet, you must be adaptable to the will of God. You need to be complementary and suitable. As you become suitable, changes will manifest in your life. When I realized how much I needed to surrender, it was difficult to fathom how much more I would have to relinquish to become suitable. I pondered how much more I'd need to sacrifice. However, God continued removing things

I needed to let go of, and I had to learn to trust Him and believe in His Word.

When God takes something away, He does so not merely to deprive but to enable growth and maturity. He transforms those situations for my benefit. What the devil intended for harm in my life, God turned around for my advantage, and I offer my praise to Him. At first, I sulked and resisted when He started taking things away from me. I protested fervently. Eventually, I reached a point where I understood that God would never ask me to surrender something without intending to turn it around for my benefit.

God reminded me a few years ago that I did not lose anything; I sowed it. He recalled to me times when I believed and persisted in that belief. I trusted Him when there was nothing visible. I held onto God's spoken word even in the absence of manifestation. Therefore, I want to encourage you to have faith in God beyond mere manifestation because you are going to be disciplined and self-controlled. I had to firmly establish in my mind that I wouldn't relent. I had to decide not to release what I learned, as someone would listen and learn from it. I am determined not to allow the Word of God to be discredited or fall into reproach by withholding what I have learned or not sharing the challenges and intricacies of my relationship.

I can testify to how good God has been through it all. I want to be candid about my mistakes. There were instances when God requested something of me, and I initially refused. I had to collect myself and offer an apology. I also want to be transparent about how I dismissed my Husband, thinking I had the right to speak to him disrespectfully in response to his disrespect toward me. However, the devil is a deceiver, and I am resolved to expose every scheme the enemy employed. I pray that anyone who listens will develop discipline and embrace sound doctrine. This is my responsibility and my sacred service.

Woman of God, you are suitable, adaptable, and complementary. You will not slow down in this role, and you will not give up. You will obey the Word of God and heed His requests. You will seek the necessary help to follow the instructions you've been given. Giving up on God's instructions is not an option, and remaining ignorant of His instructions is also not acceptable. You must study and accomplish it. You must heal so you can hear God's Word and His instructions, and then you must grow strong enough to obey them. There is no alternative. You heal to hear, and you grow strong enough to obey. Once you heal sufficiently to hear God's will, Word, way, and instructions, everything else will fall into place. When we follow God's instructions, everything else aligns. This doesn't guarantee continuous ease, nor does it mean immediate results. You'll need more self-control and discipline, but remember that obedience is superior to sacrifice. God's instructions are not negotiable, and when you start thinking otherwise, it's a sign that you need more strength and discipline. It indicates the need for more self-control, understanding, and healing. But don't stop until you attain it. Pursue it diligently. Do not become weary in doing good (Galatians 6:9). Overcome weariness; overpower tiredness; crush it, and obliterate it. Speak strength immediately with authority, power, and knowledge, in accordance with God's Word.

Discover what is written in the Word of God and declare it. Hold onto it. Rather than clutching onto weariness, brokenness, tiredness, frustration, and anger, discover what is written and practice self-control. Align yourself immediately with the principles of the Bible and surround yourself with individuals who are doing the same. When your flesh desires weariness and surrender, you don't need to hear those same words from people around you. Such words can burden you like a brick. Be cautious during this season about the company you keep. Be selective about who speaks into your life as you require strength from God. Foolishness doesn't provide strength. Lies don't provide strength. Ignorance doesn't provide strength. These elements drain your strength and deplete you. If you find yourself wondering why you're depleted, examine what you're allowing into your ears. Check what you're watching. The enemy's task is to steal your strength, but the Bible teaches that the joy of the Lord is your strength (Nehemiah 8:10). Reclaim your joy and command it to surface.

As we conclude this chapter, I want to declare Amos 9:13-15 over you: "Yes indeed, it won't be long now. God's Decree. Things are going to happen so fast your head will swim, one thing fast on the heels of the other. You won't be able to keep up. Everything will be happening at once—and everywhere you look, blessings! Blessings like wine pouring off the mountains and hills. I'll make everything right again for my people" (MSG).

In a world where the search for "good men" is a common refrain, let's shift the focus to a

different question: "Where are all the good Helpmeets?" This often overlooked role holds vital importance, yet resources on it are scarce compared to information about weddings and being a wife. The next section of this book aims to bridge that gap and guide you on the journey of becoming a Helpmeet.

In the upcoming chapters, I will share my experiences in learning this essential truth: Being a Helpmeet requires active preparation, self-reflection, and healing from past hurts. It is a divine assignment bestowed upon us by God, often overshadowed in families, churches, and communities. Through my personal journey and the transformative power of revelation, I offer guidance on embracing this role with submission, obedience, and a willingness to undergo specialized training.

Join me as we delve into the multifaceted nature of a Helpmeet and explore practical ways to embody its attributes. Discover the significance of adaptability, suitability, and complementarity, as well as the crucial role of the Holy Spirit in our marriages. Whether you're unmarried or already a Helpmeet, this book will inspire purpose, healing, and a deeper understanding of God's love in your relationship.

Are you ready for this life-altering journey? Let's embark on the path of fulfillment and transformation together.

HELPMEET JOURNAL ENTRY

1. What is God saying to you after reading this chapter?
2. What are some prayer targets you need to add?

∼

_____

_____

_____

_____

_____

_____

_____

_____

_____

_____

_____

_____

_____

_____

_____

_____

_____

_____

_____

6
HELPMEET...THE HARDEST JOB WITH NO TRAINING

YOU GOT THE JOB

Being a Helpmeet is perhaps the most challenging role any wife can undertake, and yet it often comes without formal training. But fear not, for a training class is now in session! As you read this book, the Holy Spirit will provide you with the necessary training to become a Helpmeet Suitable. Just like any job, you can't excel until you've received proper training and guidance from an instructor. Through my own journey, God has equipped me to teach this subject directly. It's an honor for me to impart this revelation and information to others.

My understanding of the Helpmeet role was quite different when I first got married. I believed that saying "I do" and having a Husband were all the qualifications I needed to fulfill my role as a Helpmeet correctly. But let me tell you, there is much more to this role than meets the eye.

Why is the role of the Helpmeet often difficult to comprehend in our society? It's because being a Helpmeet is a Kingdom principle. It doesn't align with the portrayal we see on television. It doesn't resemble the ideal we may have dreamed of as children. It's not as simple as it may seem; it demands effort. We often become disheartened because the marriage we anticipated to be a fairytale turns out to be more like a circus. There are no fairytale marriages. However, this doesn't mean that marriage can't be exciting and joyful. It doesn't mean our spouses won't show love. What it does mean is that we have a responsibility to carry out our roles according to God's plan, regardless of the situation or circumstances.

The role of the Helpmeet is so vital that the training should begin long before the vows of "I do" are exchanged. Unfortunately, it's often during times of turmoil or counseling that we realize we haven't adequately prepared ourselves to handle this monumental task.

There's a rising presence of women in ministry, business, and influential roles within our society. However, this doesn't negate the fact that God has called us to be submissive in our homes. God is using women in powerful ways, and this trend shows no signs of slowing down. The *chayil* woman is on the rise as a symbol of strength. In Hebrew, "chayil" signifies one who is anointed with strength, wisdom, virtue, power, wealth, and might. Women are making significant contributions in ministry, witnessing miracles, signs, and wonders. Prophecies are being fulfilled even as we speak. We observed this in some of the 2018 elections and within the body of Christ. Yet, this doesn't alter the Word of God regarding women's roles in our homes and alongside our Husbands.

If we fail to align ourselves with our assignments, we might miss out on what God is orchestrating in our lives. We could overlook important blessings and instructions due to disorder in our homes. We must operate within the divine order of God so that we can fulfill the purpose He has called us to in His Kingdom.

God is many things, but chaos is not among them. He is a God of order, and His decisions are unwavering. Therefore, if you're called to marriage, even during separation, and God has instructed you to mend your marital bond, then you must persevere for the sake of your family. If you stand in the gap or if your Husband is not fully transformed, do not abandon him or your destiny. Isaiah 55:11 proclaims, "So shall My word be that goes forth out of My mouth: it shall not return to Me void [without producing any effect, useless], but it shall accomplish that which I please and purpose, and it shall prosper in the things for which I sent it" (AMPC). Rely on the Word of God and fulfill the tasks He has designated for you. To see God's Word yield results, we must live by it. As Helpmeets, we must understand the principles and strategies that govern our role going forward. I will elaborate on these in the upcoming chapters.

Submission is also a pivotal subject and a key attribute of a Helpmeet. Submission exemplifies respect and humility. God expects Helpmeets to submit to their Husbands. This proves to be a challenge for many women who are leaders in their own right. Yet, there exists a scriptural approach to usher God into your household and facilitate change and improvement. To fulfill our biblical duties as Helpmeets, respect and honor must be purposeful. I must admit that I lacked the know-how as a strong woman to achieve this. While I was proficient at effecting change in my workplace and church, when adversity struck my home, I had to adhere consistently to the strategies God instructed me to employ. I exercised my authority and commanded the enemy to depart from my home because I understood my role and its associated power.

When I learned how to submit to my Husband, I also learned how to respect him, regardless of his actions. I understand it might be hard to believe I said "whatever he does," but the clarity will come as you read further. For instance, God may have called you into ministry, but it seems as if He isn't concerned about whether your Husband is saved, needs deliverance, or is fulfilling his role as a Husband. Trust me; there is hope, for nothing is impossible through Christ. There was a time when my Husband struggled with drug addiction, and God asked me to stand in the gap and intercede for him while continuing in ministry. I might not have respected his behavior or actions, but God's Word commanded that I respect him. Once we make up our minds and align ourselves with the Word of God, we can anticipate God's intervention. When God steps in, miracles can happen.

Did I initially believe this was possible? No, but I certainly believe it now because I witnessed it. When I stepped aside, became still before the Lord, and submitted myself, I observed God rescuing my Husband from the clutches of the enemy. I personally experienced God's healing in my life, enabling me to grow spiritually as I allowed God to take the lead. As you progress through the upcoming pages, ask yourself this question: what does God's job description for a Helpmeet entail?

ARE YOU READY FOR THE JOB?

Helpmeets assist, come beside their Husbands, and complete them. It is a role that requires much prayer and time with God, as well as an obedient heart. God bless our mothers, but they may not have had a lot of training or understanding of a Helpmeet. Others may not have had parents who were married. We may not have had an example of a Helpmeet while growing up. Often, we look to leaders in our society, culture, and/or the church, but we do not necessarily see a true godly example of a Kingdom marriage. Instead, we're witnessing what people have become comfortable with and have grown complacent about in marriage.

As I studied the Helpmeet role, what I saw and thought was right was not necessarily what God ordered. When I petitioned God, I realized my own life was not lining up with His Word. I asked God in prayer what he meant by asking me to be a Helpmeet Suitable. I thought to myself, "I'm home every day. I go to church. I'm saved, and I have a career." Basically, I believed I was a Proverbs 31 woman, but that was not sufficient for the warfare I was experiencing in my home. God said, "Yvette, you need to be the Helpmeet that Gerald needs. There are specific things that he needs, and if you allow Me, I will help you become suitable." Do you know I was extremely offended? Let me be transparent. When God responded, I asked, "What do you mean?" I told God, "I do this. I do that; I do more than what I think some other people do." The Lord told me, "But I need you to be suitable, and that means whatever your Husband needs. I placed what you need in you before you were placed in your mother's womb because I knew you would be with him. I created you to be with him, and there are some strategic tools inside you to help him accomplish his purpose. However, you are not using them properly, and one of those tools is being a Helpmeet Suitable."

God also impressed upon me the importance of being submitted and how to follow and encourage my Husband to lead. God taught me that if he's doing this, be quiet. If he's doing that, pray for him. If he's not acting right, continue to do as God directs. So many people thought I was crazy, but truthfully, I was obedient. According to Genesis 2:21, we come from the side of the man. We are a part of our Husbands and have been called alongside them. Some may ask what to do if their Husbands never get saved or ever change. What if they never do right? Does God still expect them to do all this? When I had the same questions, God reminded me of the sacrifice of Jesus. He said, "I asked My Son Jesus to give up His life. I am asking you to sacrifice as well." I realized it was like Jesus asking God why He should have to give up His life without the guarantee that everyone would be saved and choose to serve Him. Of course, Jesus did not say that. Christ knew He wanted to please the Father and declared He would give up His will for the will of the Father. To fulfill His destiny, it did not matter whether one person or several million people got saved. Jesus knew He was to do what the Father asked of Him.

If you are not willing to put in the work or you are looking for an easy way out, being a Helpmeet Suitable will not be possible. You must trust and understand that the Word of God works, and it will not return void. Therefore, it is imperative that your life lines up with the Word to have the power through God to accomplish becoming suitable. God expects us to be an example of His Word. Allow Him to use you for His glory in your home and let your spouse see, feel, and hear God through you. We must renew our minds to realize that regardless of our spouses' actions, God will only hold us accountable for our actions. Our focus is to hear our Master say, "Well done, good and faithful servant" (Matthew 25:23).

In Proverbs 18:21 the Bible says, "Death and life are in the power of the tongue, and they who indulge in it shall eat of it [for death or life]" (AMPC). Because you have a covenant with your Husband, you can speak life into him and cause the atmosphere in your home to change. Until his deliverance comes, and you see a manifestation of your prayers, be an example and a living epistle of obedience. Pray for him and show him the agape love of God.

HELPMEET JOURNAL ENTRY

1. What is God saying to you after reading this chapter?
2. What are some prayer targets you need to add?

∾

_____

_____

_____

_____

_____

_____

_____

_____

_____

_____

_____

_____

_____

_____

_____

_____

_____

_____

7

HELPMEET: SHIFT WITH THE HOLY SPIRIT

"But the Helper (Comforter, Advocate, Intercessor—
Counselor, Strengthener, Standby), the Holy
Spirit, whom the Father will send in My name
[in My place, to represent Me and act on My
behalf], He will teach you all things. And He
will help you remember everything that I have
told you" (John 14:26).

There's a shift in the spiritual atmosphere in this season. Along with that shift, God desires to see the family unit move as well. However, the enemy's plan is to hinder Husbands and Helpmeets from hearing and obeying the Holy Spirit. God will not excuse us from the things He has asked based on the behavior or habits of our spouses. That's why it's crucial to be able to hear the Holy Spirit. We must remember that the Bible doesn't provide instructions to Helpmeets only when our Husbands make a certain amount of money, honor their vows, or fulfill our perceived expectations. The Bible clearly outlines instructions for both Husbands and Helpmeets regarding the intended operation of marriage roles. However, neither spouse is exempt from these expectations based on their partner's behavior. This understanding was challenging for me to grasp. I frequently asked the Holy Spirit to lead and guide me in learning how to treat my Husband in alignment with God's expectations, rather than treating him according to what I believed he deserved.

When I truly understood that God wanted me to invest more time in obeying His Word than trying to hold my Husband accountable, I experienced a breakthrough in my spiritual growth. In essence, I had enough to learn on my own. The Holy Spirit taught me to entrust my Husband to Him. Study the attributes of the Holy Spirit to gain a better understanding of a helper.

HELPMEET, THE COMFORTER

According to Webster's dictionary, a comforter is defined as someone who "gives strength and hope, eases grief or trouble." Whenever Husbands are dealing with challenges requiring this skill, we as Helpmeets are created to provide comfort to them, much like the role of the Holy Spirit. We mustn't seize the opportunity to become a "foolish woman" and tear them down; instead, we should rise as wise women and uplift them. This is a chance to deposit love, trust, and faith into our Husbands. Hopefully, the next time they face difficulties, they'll be more willing to share their feelings and concerns. Be the comforter your Husband can rely on.

HELPMEET, THE ADVOCATE

If you have ever been to court to testify or assisted someone who made a poor decision, you may have had to speak on their behalf.

This is the central role of an advocate. As an advocate for your Husband, you represent him and, on occasion, speak on his behalf. One way we advocate for our Husbands is by reminding the enemy they have been redeemed by the blood of the Lamb, Jesus Christ. In 1 John 2:1, Jesus says, "My little children (believers, dear ones), I am writing you these things so that you will not sin and violate God's law. And if anyone sins, we have an Advocate [who will intercede for us] with the Father: Jesus Christ the righteous [the upright, the just One, who conforms to the Father's will in every way, purpose, thought, and action)" (AMP).

Just as Jesus Christ advocated for us, we must also be advocates and stand in the gap for our Husbands. Have you ever had someone share something negative about a friend or family member? Even if what the person said was true, did you defend your friend or relative or did you join in? We must work diligently to advocate on behalf of our Husbands. Stand by your man!

HELPMEET, THE INTERCESSOR

God has equipped us tremendously. Not only are we comforters and advocates, but we are also intercessors. An intercessor brings a need before God and stands in the gap. Take the time to ask your Husband, "Are you struggling at work or having trouble finding work? Are you struggling with salvation or deliverance? Is anything troubling you?" Once we have the answers, we are to intercede. Go to God and petition His help on behalf of your Husband. Don't pray for God to change his behavior based on your feelings or needs. Instead, pray for God's perfect will for his life. Also ask God, "What can I do for him? How can I intercede and stand in the gap for my Husband?" God will give you prayer strategies that can powerfully impact your lives.

Being an intercessor does not mean we start praying for our Husbands to do things the way we want them done. We cannot misuse intercession. Doing so would constitute manipulation, which is witchcraft. We are not to use prayer to manipulate. Furthermore, as an intercessor and advocate, do not let anyone speak negatively about your Husband. If someone speaks against your Husband, walk away or shut it down. Do not engage in the conversation. I've learned to take a stand: no one speaks negatively about my Husband, especially not me. Life and death are in the power of the tongue (Proverbs 18:21). During times of challenging marital problems, people would tell me, "Your Husband is doing this or that." As hurtful as those statements were, I had to use wisdom. As I grew spiritually and in my role as my Husband's intercessor, I learned to respond by saying, "Pray for him!" Discussing it further would breathe life into the actions, and I refused to give the enemy a foothold in our lives.

As intercessors, we want to build a relationship where our Husbands can come to us and speak freely about what they are dealing with. Consider if you went to the Holy Spirit and said, "I need help. I need strength," and the Holy Spirit responded, "Not right now. I'm a little busy helping Sister so-and-so." The Holy Spirit would never respond to anyone in this way. Therefore, our responses to our Husbands should be helpful and affirming.

HELPMEET, THE STRENGTHENER

The Husband is the leader and head of the home but if he is struggling with his past, emotions, addictions, or habits, you are the strengthener. When my Husband and I were facing significant challenges in our marriage, I was expecting him to be the strengthener. I kept saying to Gerald, "What are you going to do about this or that?" I'm sure many of us have been in this situation. We want our Husbands to handle whatever comes our way, and God had to guide me. After realizing that the issues weren't changing, I turned to prayer. God said, "You're right. He's supposed to address this and that. But what could you have done to assist him in handling it? Could you have been more understanding? Could you have suggested praying together? Could you have offered some encouraging words?"

Strengtheners never tear down; their purpose is to build up. The enemy will attempt to use a Helpmeet to hinder her Husband if she's not careful. Many will encounter similar challenges, but God is seeking those who will step out in faith and break this cycle. If you find yourself unintentionally working against your Husband due to the enemy's influence, quickly apologize to him and seek forgiveness from God. Remind your Husband that you two are united. A few years ago, a Prophet spoke a word into our lives. She said, "You two have each other's back. It's like the two of you are standing back to back." Given all we've experienced and navigated in our marriage, this was reassuring for both of us because we haven't always maintained this perspective.

I challenge you to ask yourself, "Do I have my Husband's back?" It's also vital to understand how your Husband would respond to that question.

HELPMEET, THE STANDBY

Some women stand stronger by men who are not their Husbands than some Helpmeets do for their Husbands. This is completely unacceptable! Helpmeets must stand by their Husbands. Our goal is to support them as the Holy Spirit supports us. Let's revisit John 14:26:

"But the Advocate, the Holy Spirit, whom the Father will send in my name, will teach you all things and will remind you of everything I have said to you."

We represent the same Holy Spirit Jesus promised to send to us. We are that help. One thing that often prevents a Helpmeet from standing by her Husband is hurt. At times, our Husbands are among those who have hurt us. God wants us to bring our feelings, worries, and cares to Him. He desires to heal us so we can fulfill His will. God's Word instructs us to pray for those who mistreat us and to forgive, or else we will not be overlooked (Matthew 5:44). This isn't easy, so we must develop the habit of asking the Holy Spirit to handle the discomfort and anger. God rewards those who diligently seek Him (Hebrews 11:6). If we believe God has brought our marital union together, then we need to be positioned to operate as the Helpmeet.

When the helper is out of place, there's more room for things to fall apart and become disorderly. For instance, have you ever used an object to prop something up? If the object suddenly moves, everything leaning on it comes crashing down. Similarly, when Helpmeets are out of place and our Husbands need support, we end up falling because they have nothing to lean on. What God has ordained as the Husband's support isn't strong enough to be leaned on. As Helpmeets, we must be strong enough to support our Husbands. This doesn't mean we're flawless, but we should seek God's strength to become stronger over time. During your prayer time, be honest and talk to God about your needs and feelings. I often start by saying, "It was hard to be kind today. It was hard not to be hurtful today. It was hard not to respond in anger today." After expressing my feelings, I can gather myself and begin to heal.

I encourage every current or future Helpmeet to have a like-minded prayer partner. We all need a prayer partner who will go to battle with us without judgment, regardless of the state of our marriages. This should be a woman you can approach with transparency and say, "I need your help," or "It's been difficult to pray for him this week." I strongly recommend that both married and unmarried women have prayer partners, as the prayer needs and strategies can differ based on marital status.

HELPMEET, THE COUNSELOR

Another critical role for a Helpmeet is that of a counselor. You might be wondering, "How can I counsel? I've never been trained or gone to school for this." The Word of the Lord in Luke 12:12 says, "For the Holy Spirit will teach you in that very hour what you ought to say." Trust the Holy Spirit to guide you in choosing the right words and attitude, making it easier for your Husband to receive your counsel. When your Husband seeks comfort or advice, you and the Holy Spirit should be there to provide guidance. Your words should uplift him and be truthful but delivered in a way that's easy to accept. Even if he disagrees, he will remember how your words were presented.

Proverbs 16:24 says, "Pleasant words are like a honeycomb, Sweet and delightful to the soul and healing to the body." Your Husband should be able to confide in you with his deepest secrets. He should feel that by speaking to you, his words remain confidential between you and God in prayer. When your spouse shares something with you, remember that he trusts you not to mock, belittle, or use it against him in an argument. The trust your Husband places in you should mirror the confidence you have in God. Beyond appreciating your Husband's trust, appreciate the trust God has in you. God believes you can handle the challenges your Husband faces. The problem arises when we choose not to face them. Just as we provide strength to our Husbands, we must let God be our strength as well. When we turn to God, we can trust that He will provide us with the comfort and strength needed to move to the next level of breakthrough, deliverance, and healing.

In John 14:16-18, Jesus says, "I will ask the Father, and He will give you another Helper, that He may be with you forever; that is the Spirit of truth, whom the world cannot receive because it does not see Him or know Him, but you know Him because He abides with you and will be in you. I will not leave you as orphans; I will come to you."

God calls all of us to become better Helpmeets. As wives, our role is to be the best Helpmeets we can be. The responsibility of future wives is to unite in prayer, supporting each other to become the best Helpmeets possible. God has positioned you to be a helper, an intercessor, a strengthener, and a counselor. Consider it a source of joy (James 1:2) as God has placed you in your Husband's life for this very purpose.

STEP UP TO THE CHALLENGE

I strongly encourage you to develop the habit of praying for your Husband without ceasing (1 Thessalonians 5:17). I challenge you to bring your concerns about your marriage to God in prayer. As you pause to listen to God, He will also show you aspects of yourself. Recognize that none of us are perfect. Your Husband might be doing things that cause concern or bother you, but the Holy Spirit can help you perceive those concerns from a different perspective. Be prepared for God to ask, "Are you fulfilling what I've asked of you?" Instead of continually presenting our spouses' actions before God, we need to inquire, "How can I shift, change, or respond differently?" This doesn't assign blame to us. Each of us has the choice to serve God or not. However, God desires to work through us to assist our Husbands in becoming all He created them to be. We should aim to treat them with love, respect, honor, and God's unconditional love. These actions will undeniably encourage them to draw closer to God. Witnessing and experiencing the genuine love of God is difficult to resist. Aim to be the embodiment of the Bible your Husband reads.

HELPMEET JOURNAL ENTRY

1. What is God saying to you after reading this chapter?
2. What are some prayer targets you need to add?

~

_____

_____

_____

_____

_____

_____

_____

_____

_____

_____

_____

_____

_____

_____

_____

_____

_____

_____

_____

8

HELPMEET SUITABLE

God is concerned about what happens in our marriages and families. He will not change His mind about the order of the home He established in His Word. I am learning more and more that regardless of my having three college degrees, a very successful career, and a calling in my life, God has an established order in my home. I am proud of my accomplishments in my career and the body of Christ. However, when I come home, I am Gerald's Helpmeet, not his pastor or teacher. I submit to and honor him. When I find myself doing disrespectful things, God quickly reminds me of His Word. I apologize and correct myself. I often hear, "He is the head of the home" from God, and it keeps me focused and humble. I frequently declare that Gerald is the Priest, Prophet, and King. God was very adamant about teaching me how He wanted me to grow and understand that respecting Gerald was extremely important to fulfilling my destiny as a woman of God. It is one of the most challenging things I have ever done, and it tested my faith, but the rewards of being in God's perfect will outweigh the struggle. I encourage you to ask God for the strength to carry out His plan, and He will provide it.

Genesis 2:18 states, "The Lord God said, 'It is not good or beneficial for the man to be alone; therefore, He made him a helper suitable.'" We were created to be helpers. God helped me understand that I was not made to lead in my house; I was made to be the helper. Truthfully, I was operating outside of His will every time I overstepped. Due to my disobedience, I experienced turmoil in my household. God wants to make us helpers who will bring balance to our Husbands. This will make us suitable and complementary to them. What I do should always complement my Husband.

It is important to know that your Husband or future Husband has specific needs that you were made to assist him with. This can mean your skills and gifts might be very different from those of other Helpmeets as what they have is specially designed for their Husbands. It is a blessing to know that I am specifically designed with everything I need to be suitable for Gerald. When you become a Helpmeet Suitable, you provide what is required to help your Husband be the Priest, Prophet, and King God has called him to be. Understand that God took the rib from the Husband and created you to complete him.

Reflecting on the past, I had my own agenda and thoughts about what my Husband needed, and I was stuck in my daily routine. God needed to teach me a new way. At that time, my Husband was dealing with drugs and depression. He was also struggling with pornography addiction. The Lord specifically told me that my Husband needed love, support, and respect from me. I told God that I supported him. After all, I was keeping the household going, and I didn't kick him out of the house. I thought that was support. With everything he was doing, I didn't know what to support. I argued with God and asked Him why He would want me to respect a man who was not doing His will and was living in sin. It made no sense to me. God said, "I made you a Helpmeet Suitable." God told me to use my authority and words to speak what I wanted to see in my Husband. I was to respect my Husband until I saw respectful behavior. I was to treat him like a King, like the man I knew God had called him to be. I declared it until it came forth. God was training me to use the power that was inside of me. God trained me to combat devils and use my spiritual warfare strategies. I learned to rebuke the devil and love Gerald.

My prayer is that more Helpmeets can see that God has made us to complement our Husbands. We have the power to shift and affect our environments. If your Husband is not doing all that God has called him to do, ask God to show you what you have on the inside to help. Your Husband still has free will. We know that God will never force His children to serve Him. However, when a Helpmeet is applying God's principles and operating in her authority, all while using her helper gifts, her Husband is far more likely to see God in her and desire to serve Him. The role God has asked you to fulfill is extremely important. One thing that shocked me as someone who was created to help is that I am either going to help the enemy devour my Husband or help God deliver my Husband. I chose to help God deliver. Our words are weapons. We can hinder our Husbands more than any other person on this earth. Our words can hinder our Husbands faster because we are in covenant with them. In Proverbs 14:1 the Word of God says, "Every wise woman builds her house, but the foolish one tears it down" (AMPC).

I learned that I must be intentional about not helping the enemy and causing more problems for Gerald. I am committed to becoming his help, not his hindrance. Very often when I counsel women, they admit they had no idea what the Helpmeet role was or how much work it entailed. Very quickly, we realize that most pre-marriage counseling never taught or prepared us for this. It's more than raising kids, being the best dressed, the ring, the wedding, or whatever the case may be. We need to be trained if we are going to be Helpmeets Suitable that please God. No doubt this is the hardest, most demanding, and most challenging job you will ever do. However, in the end, the reward will be worth it.

We want God to say to us, "Well done, my good and faithful servant" (Matthew 25:23). This is exactly what I needed and wanted to hear. I wanted God to be proud of me. Once you truly understand what the Word says, you will see why what God says is so important. Even if you don't know what your Husband is doing, how long it will take for him to get off drugs, or how long the affair will be, know that we can do all things through Christ. Trust me when I say that I am in no way excusing or condoning sin. Sin is and always will be completely wrong. What we must understand is that our job as Helpmeets is to love our Husbands through sin and allow God to convict and deal with sinful behavior. Vengeance belongs to the Lord (Deuteronomy 32:35), and there are wages to sin. This was very difficult for me to understand because I was very good at bringing Gerald's sin before the Lord. Every time I mentioned Gerald's sin, the Holy Spirit either said, "Be still and know that I am God" (Psalm 46:10) or brought my attention to how wrong my responses to my Husband were. God caused me to focus more on my spiritual responses and growth than allowing me to focus on the wrong Gerald was doing. Ironically, it was the love and respect that drew Gerald back to Christ, and that is when the sin was dealt with. Basically, I learned to let God deal with it because He does it best.

I used to think if I could just preach the scriptures, it would cause Gerald to be convicted of his sin. This practice damaged our relationship and caused his heart to become hardened against the will of God. Our communication became non-existent, and it put a strain on our marriage. Many nights in prayer, God would tell me to be quiet, but I just continued to badger Gerald with the Word. What God wanted from me was to live the Word in front of him, to become a living Epistle. This caused far more of a reaction than any sermon I ever preached in our home. I knew how to preach sermons in a pulpit, but God told me to leave the pulpit at church. When I got home, I was to put on my "suitable" clothes, submit, respect, and become complementary to my Husband.

Marriage is indeed a lot of work, but it's worth it when we are doing what God has called us to do. The foundation must be the Word of God. We must continually ask ourselves, "Are my life and attitude lining up with the Word? Am I a Helpmeet Suitable?" I'm not a finished product. I'm all about the perfecting of the saints. Through resources, individuals, and most importantly, the Word of God, we're going to be suitable. We're going to learn this because the devil often uses us to hinder our Husbands, and we don't even know it. The time for that is over! We must truly understand that:

RESPECT + SUBMISSION = A HELPMEET SUITABLE.

HELPMEET JOURNAL ENTRY

1. What is God saying to you after reading this chapter?
2. What are some prayer targets you need to add?

~

9

A SANCTIFIED WIFE SANCTIFIES THE HUSBAND

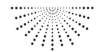

L ife has a way of throwing curveballs at us, and you may feel as if you have been hit by one that has caused your marriage to bend or hit you, but declare from your mouth that it has not broken you. God is and was there through it all.

Hebrews 13:5 states, "For He [God] Himself has said, I will not in any way fail you nor give you up nor leave you without support. [I will] not, [I will] not, [I will] not in any degree leave you helpless nor forsake nor let [you] down (relax My hold on you)! [Assuredly not!]" (AMPC). In my marriage, my Husband was struggling and needed deliverance. During the time we were separated, he was dealing with addictions and generational curses that were attacking him. Now, when I share our testimony, people often ask me, "Why did you hold on? How did you endure it for so long? What were you thinking?" These are all questions that I asked myself in the beginning when I started the process, but God was with me the whole time.

If your spouse is not present, whether physically and/or emotionally, it may seem impossible at the time to believe in God for restoration. I have spoken to people over the last few years and ministered to many wives and, at times, the Husbands as well. Often, a spouse is holding on through challenges like adultery, addictions, and lack of commitment. I can wholeheartedly relate to the fact that it can be extremely challenging. "Yet, in these things, we are more than conquerors and gain an overwhelming victory through Him who loved us [so much that He dies for us]" (Romans 8:37).

BE STRENGTHENED, BE CREATIVE, BE A FIGHTER

God will always strengthen us when we ask for help. According to Psalms 46:1, "The Holy Spirit is our strength and present help in the time of trouble." Be encouraged in this season and continue to ask the Holy Spirit to give you the strength to hold on daily. Your marriage is worth saving, no matter what it looks like now.

During the time that we were struggling in our relationship, God asked me to be prepared and sanctify my home. As I was praying, I asked: "Lord, what do you want me to do?"

God said, "Create an atmosphere that is conducive to deliverance." He admonished me to speak His Word over His son, my Husband. After all he had done and was still doing, God continued to call him His son. Then, God said, "Would you ever allow the enemy to come into your home and take your son and not put up a fight?"

I immediately said, "You know how I feel about my son. I would never permit the enemy to come in and take my child!"

God then asked, "What would you do?"

I quickly responded, "I'd fight, pray, and fast for him!"

Then God said something that rocked me to my core. He said, "You allowed the enemy to come into your home and take My son. You didn't fight for Gerald."

I had to take a step back and admit—I'm not fighting for Gerald. I was hurt and honestly embarrassed at the reality of what I had just heard. I was so bothered by my personal feelings and circumstances I didn't think about the fact that I needed to fight for Gerald as my Husband. The Lord reminded me quickly that a sanctified wife sanctifies the Husband and the sanctified Husband sanctifies the wife (1 Corinthians 7:14).

Gerald and I were in a spiritual war, but this was a war I could win with God's help. So, I asked God to give me the strength to fight the way He wanted me to fight. I knew I needed resources to help me. I went to the bookstore, purchased a book on spiritual warfare, and began to study. As I researched this topic, I started to believe verses such as 2 Timothy 2:3-4, which say, "Take with me your share of hardship (passing through the difficulties which are called to endure), like a good soldier of Christ Jesus. No soldier in active service gets entangled in the (ordinary business) affairs of civilian life; (he avoids them) so that he may please the one who enlisted him to serve." Wow, I was in for a significant shift in my spiritual life.

DECLARE IT!

The Lord asked me to write down everything that was ever prophesied about my Husband, his gifts, and his destiny. We have had the privilege of having been prayed for by some very powerful men and women of God. The Lord said, "Who did they say Gerald was? How did they describe him? Speak it to me in your prayer time." I remembered that Gerald had been called an apostolic leader and a Prophet. He has an anointing to minister the gospel and operate in miracles and healing. Truthfully, because of the hurt and some of the things that were going on in our relationship, it was hard to remember so many great things that had been said about him. Despite this, God said, "Write them down and declare them." I've learned if you're doing anything that requires change, you must come up with a strategy to help you complete it. So, I wrote down everything about him. He was a coach, a mentor, and a teacher. I continued to write down things God said Gerald was, and I began to speak them. After a few days, it got a little easier because I started to believe who my Husband is.

- He is a strong and faithful man of God.
- He is the Priest, Prophet, and King of our home.
- He is a Kingdom Man, a Kingdom Husband, and a Kingdom Father.
- He has the anointing for entrepreneurship.

I kept speaking these things, and then God asked me to find scriptures I could use to help me have faith in the anointing and gifts he possessed. This made it even easier to fight for him. It also helped me begin to respect and honor him.

> **Strategy**: What are some of the titles of your Husband? The Bible instructs us to call those things that are not as though they are (Romans 4:17), so speak over your Husband. Write down what God says about him. When you realize who God has connected you with, who you are in a covenant with, and who God has designed specifically for you, your eyes will begin to open. I realized that Gerald is a man with an anointing on his life. He is a man with a destiny and a purpose to be great, and God entrusted him to me as his Helpmeet. God trusted that I would

fight for Gerald and pray over him. Fighting for my Husband was part of what I agreed to do when I became his Helpmeet.

DECLARE WHO GOD CREATED YOUR HUSBAND TO BE

This process became my passion. I found books to read that taught me about my Husband's gifts and purpose. For example, it has been prophesied that Gerald has the gift of healing. So, I had to find books that were about Gerald's gift of healing, take information from the books, and declare it over his life.

Strategy: Develop a system that helps you stay consistent in keeping track of what you learn about your Husband's gifts, as the Bible says that our tongues can become the pen of a ready writer (Psalm 45:1).

This strategy is key to becoming a Helpmeet Suitable. It is useful for a person who has a great marriage and wants to keep it great. It is also for those who feel they are at the end of the rope concerning their marriages. I know that feeling all too well. I have been on my knees asking God for help, saying, "You have to give me the strength because I don't feel I can go one more day holding onto this marriage or this man." As God gave me the strength, I continued to write things down. I continued to look up scriptures that addressed who Gerald was as a Kingdom man. Every time I spoke those scriptures, I gained more strength to keep fighting.

I continued to speak scriptures over Gerald, even while we were separated. After Gerald returned home, he told me about a specific day and time when he honestly thought the devil was trying to kill him. As we compared dates, I realized it was the same day I had been on my knees speaking over him pleading for his deliverance. I could literally feel a tug of war happening, so I continued to say, "He is a Priest, Prophet, and King." The Word of God says, "Faith come by hearing and hearing by the Word of God" (Romans 10:17). I looked up the scripture and declared it specifically. I declared who God said Gerald was.

Strategy: Declare out loud the characteristics of your Husband based on what you learn from the Bible. It may seem like a simple thing, but when you are hurt and you don't see proper behavior, it is challenging. Nevertheless, it is worth the fight.

There were nights I resisted reading those declarations. It seemed like a waste of time at first. Begrudgingly, I began to program myself to read that list out loud before I went to sleep. I learned I was not just reading to myself. Rather, I was putting these declarations in the atmosphere and decreeing a thing, so that I could rest, knowing it was established just as the Bible says (Job 22:28). I was decreeing and declaring, and then after a while, it became a prayer. Later it became a war cry. I was in my room; my kids were asleep, and I was making statements about Gerald out loud. Eventually, the list started to grow because as my heart softened, I would remember other prophecies, strengths, and gifts. When I thought of another title or another one of Gerald's gifts, I searched the Scriptures, added it to the list, and spoke it over him. I started to realize Gerald was a man of God worth fighting for. I know some will read this and say they don't have contact with their Husbands. For a very long time, I did not have contact with Gerald because we were separated. I had no idea where he was living, and he would not return any of my phone calls. As silly as this process seemed to me, God knew I needed to declare these scriptures to get them in my heart. When I was healed, delivered, and understood who God created my Husband to be, He opened the door for Gerald to return. This time,

I was ready to treat him with godly love and respect. I'll continue to say it as I share our testimony—I did not do what I did because Gerald was my Husband. I did it because God asked me to do it. We must come to a place in our relationship with God that when He asks us to do something—no matter what it sounds like—no matter what others think—no matter what it looks like—no matter what you're thinking might happen—we must be obedient.

HELPMEET JOURNAL ENTRY

1. What is God saying to you after reading this chapter?
2. What are some prayer targets you need to add?

~

_____

_____

_____

_____

_____

_____

_____

_____

_____

_____

_____

_____

_____

_____

_____

_____

_____

_____

10

BE OBEDIENT

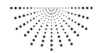

On this journey, we will be challenged by the scripture, "Obedience is better than sacrifice" (1 Samuel 15:22). God said to speak over Gerald, so I spoke! I wasn't sure if this was going to repair my relationship with my Husband, but I knew I didn't want to damage my relationship with God. Once you reach a point where you don't want to damage your relationship with God, He can trust you. I wanted God to trust me. So, I figured if I did what God asked me to do and Gerald never came home, at least I could say, "God, I did what you asked me to do. God, I want you to be pleased with me. God, I am your soldier. You gave me orders, and I followed them." Eventually, Gerald did come home, and I was able to share the list with him. He was so blessed by what he read, and it helped him begin to believe in himself. To this day, I declare over my Husband and anoint his head with oil as he sleeps.

Now, when Gerald's struggling with something, he will say, "When you're praying over me, would you pray that the scales come off my eyes or pray over my ears because I want to hear God clearly? I want to see what God is showing me because I don't want anything to hinder what God is doing." It is so vital that every Husband can be secure that his Helpmeet is truly praying for him and declaring his destiny. This strategy puts a Helpmeet in a position to cancel every assignment of the enemy that is sent to hinder our families. Now, I see my Husband operating in every gift and calling spoken over him. No one is perfect, and we both have room to grow spiritually. However, I can see the prayers coming to pass, and I can see the declarations working.

It's so exciting to witness people grow, get closer to God, and move into their destinies. Gerald was bound by addictions and generational curses of lust and perversion. He was also addicted to pornography, marijuana, and alcohol. There were several challenges he had to overcome, so I honor him for all his hard work in pursuing and maintaining his deliverance. When Gerald decided to believe God for his deliverance, he had to fight, and the declaration list became something that helped him do so. Satan attempted to deceive him, and it made it hard for him to remember who God called him to be. The Bible tells us, "My people perish for lack of knowledge" (Hosea 4:6) and "Without a vision, the people perish" (Proverbs 29:18). So, the declaration list became our vision. When life doesn't look like our declarations, or if our behavior doesn't line up with the list, we've learned to go back in and fight, pray, and say our declarations out loud.

BE STRATEGIC AND CONSISTENT

We must always pray without ceasing (1 Thessalonians 5:17). I encourage you to pray while in your car, in your prayer closet, at your job—anytime you can. Ask God for strength and direction. When a married couple becomes one, their destiny and purpose are connected. You don't want your destiny and purpose hindered because you or your spouse are not in line with God's Word and His will.

At one point, I started to worry, thinking, "What's going to happen to my destiny and purpose? What's going to happen to the ministry that I know God called me into if my Husband is on the streets or on drugs? What's going to happen if my Husband runs away from our home or leaves our house?" Now I understand. Gerald left our house because he started to feel defeated and believed he couldn't take care of things in our home, so he just walked away. God showed me he wasn't walking away from me as his wife; he was walking away from Him and His call on his life. That declaration list helped tremendously when Gerald came back because there was an atmosphere in our home that was conducive to deliverance. After our separation, Gerald returned to our home and could feel those prayers. He could tell something had changed in our home and me. Because the Husband is the head of the house, satan continually attacks him. When the head of the house is not in alignment, satan tries to bind the entire family. Satan attacked my Husband, and as his Helpmeet, I had to step up and tell him, "You cannot have my Husband, our home, or our family!" I could not tell whether my prayers or declarations were working, but out of obedience, I did it anyway.

My faith created a different atmosphere. Not only was it different, but I was different. I changed, and my heart was not hardened toward Gerald as a person. As I prayed for my Husband, God began to heal me too. I remember one day, I asked God, "Do you love him more than you love me? Why would you ask me to pray for someone who has hurt me so badly?" God replied, "Do you love Me? Sometimes you hurt Me, and your behavior hurts Me, but I still love you. I still want you to come to Me and talk to Me. You are still my daughter." I grew spiritually and realized it was not about whether God loved Gerald more than He loved me or not. God loved both of us, and He wanted our entire household to be saved and delivered. I must admit, when my Husband began living for the Lord, I slacked off on the fervency of my prayers and declarations. Before I got too comfortable, a Prophet spoke to me and reminded me that I could not stop doing the special assignment God had given me. She said, "If it worked, keep going. Those prayers are like an arrow, penetrating the atmosphere. I see this bow and arrow, and it's like you are shooting things in the spirit; don't stop." Two days later, someone challenged us to look up what our names meant. I looked up Yvette and found out it meant archer. An archer is someone who shoots a bow and arrow. I am an archer, called to fight for my marriage and destiny. So, I am decreeing and declaring that you have the strength to fight for your family too. Don't give up on your marriage, your Husband, or your children. Don't give up!

God is a miracle-working God, and He wants His children saved, set free, and delivered. The minute I asked God for help, I could feel His presence. "Just open your mouth," God said. When Gerald left and went to live in another state, he testified that he could feel God's presence all over him. He was trying to kill himself with drugs and alcohol. He said the voice of God was so loud he couldn't get drunk or high. I know that speaking out loud allowed a hedge of protection over Gerald and everything he was going through. It gave him enough strength to come home. Now, speaking declarations is our lifestyle because speaking God's Word is a key component of helping us maintain our deliverance. It allows us to focus on who we are and who God has called us to be!

HELPMEET JOURNAL ENTRY

1. What is God saying to you after reading this chapter?
2. What are some prayer targets you need to add?

～

_____

_____

_____

_____

_____

_____

_____

_____

_____

_____

_____

_____

_____

_____

_____

_____

_____

_____

11

I AM A SANCTIFIED WIFE

*"For the unbelieving Husband is sanctified [that is,
he receives the blessings granted] through his
[Christian] wife, and the unbelieving wife is
sanctified through her believing Husband.
Otherwise, your children would be
[ceremonially] unclean, but as it is, they are holy"*
(*1 Corinthians 7:14*).

Marriages are under attack by the enemy, and God desires them to be restored. God aims to work the miraculous in the earthly realm through marriage restoration. Many of these miracles will occur through the sanctified wife with the assistance of God. There will be no limits to how God can and will employ the sanctified wife. This is not to suggest that the sanctified Husband cannot also inflict significant damage on the Kingdom of darkness. However, at present, God has a call for women to undergird their Husbands, stand by them, and pray for their deliverance. I am not stating that every Husband needs major deliverance, but if your Husband is called by God, as he is, then you have work to do. We should never assume we have everything together and let our guard down. Men are the heads of the household, making them the primary targets of enemy attacks. Many families are grappling with stress, anxiety, addiction, separation, and divorce. We must wage war against marriage-breaking spirits and declare that enough is enough! They will no longer sow discord in our homes. Therefore, there is a compelling need for women, not only to come together and support one another but also to study our role as Helpmeets.

You may be saying to yourself, "I didn't sign up for this." More often than we would like to admit, many of us had no idea what we were getting into when we said, "I do." Being a Helpmeet is the godly role of a wife, and much of our helping will be done while we are also healing.

YOU WERE BUILT FOR THIS

After reading all of this, I'm sure you still have questions, and that's perfectly okay! Some of the questions you might be asking are common among many women:

- How can my sanctification change my relationship?
- Why did God ask me to stand for my marriage?
- Why do I feel as if there's so much weight on me to carry my family and to pray for my Husband to be set free?

God welcomes our questions, and He wants you to talk to Him, rather than thinking that we're in this alone. As you ask your questions, remember to tell yourself: "I was built for this."

In 1 Peter 3:1, the apostle Peter says: "In the same way, you wives, be [a]submissive to your own Husbands [subordinate, not as inferior, but out of respect for the responsibilities entrusted to Husbands and their accountability to God, and so partnering with them] so that even if some do not obey the word [of God], they may be won over [to Christ] without discussion by the godly lives of their wives."

- You were created to sanctify.
- You were created to give life.
- You were created to help!
- You are stronger than you think.

Let me encourage you to never give up. Do not stand down. We are at war with the enemy, so we must come together and understand more about our spiritual arsenal and God-ordained authority on the earth. We must know and become knowledgeable about the weapons we can use to cancel every assignment of the enemy. As it is written, the weapons of our warfare are not physical [weapons of flesh and blood]. Our weapons are divinely powerful for the destruction of fortresses (2 Corinthians 10:4). The devil will no longer have a stronghold over current or future Helpmeets. Remember, it is so important that those who are Helpmeets in waiting are doing more than just finding a venue. What they're doing is preparing themselves to be suitable and to be found. The Bible says, "He who finds a [true and faithful] wife finds a good thing. And obtains favor and approval from the Lord" (Proverbs 18:22).

When women can get together and say, "I want to know what my role is as a Helpmeet," even though they are not married, how much more powerful and prepared will women be? Women can believe God concerning this and expect their marriages will be stronger. As written in Titus 2:3-5, "Older women similarly are to be reverent in their behavior, not malicious gossips nor addicted to much wine, teaching what is right and good, so that they may encourage the young women to love their Husbands and their children tenderly, to be sensible, pure, makers of a home [where God is honored], good-natured, being subject to their own Husbands, so that the word of God will not be dishonored."

YOU'VE BEEN SET APART FOR THIS

As said before, to sanctify means to be set apart. To say this is difficult may be an understatement. So, when you feel tired, declare that you will not get weary in well-doing. You will not stop. You will not slow down because your children are watching, and your Husband needs you. Not only them, but other women need your strength too. God has called you to do a mighty work in becoming sanctified for your Husband. God wants you to know that you are not alone. Some of our Husbands are indeed hurting, and some of us are in difficult situations. But our goal is to do what God has asked us to do. We are only held accountable for what God has asked us to do as Helpmeets. Be encouraged, for the Bible says, "I can do all things [which He has called me to do] through Him who strengthens and empowers me [to fulfill His purpose—I am self-sufficient in Christ's sufficiency; I am ready for anything and equal to anything through Him who infuses me with inner strength and confident peace.]" (Philippians 4:7).

God asked me to stand firm for my Husband.

God asked me to pray for him.

God asked me to treat him like I loved him.

I had to love him as if I had never been hurt.

God said, "Let me provide you with personal strategies for your Husband." And He did just that. He delivered my Husband and saved my marriage. I'm overwhelmed with gratitude for the incredible work that God has done and continues to do in my life. I'm compelled to share my testimony with as many Helpmeets as possible. We must stand together, inspiring and guiding others so they don't lose hope. I understand the struggles, but I declare boldly over you that you are a sanctified woman, fortified with divine strength to persistently evolve in your role as a Helpmeet. You stand as a sanctified wife, and no matter how challenging the present circumstances may appear, rest assured that God not only can but will heed your fervent prayers.

The Word says what we should do in 1 Thessalonians 5:11, "Therefore encourage and comfort one another and build up one another, just as you are doing." No matter what the devil says, you can sanctify your Husband. "Continue to put on the complete armor of God, so that you will be able to successfully resist and stand your ground in the evil day" (Ephesians 6:13).

IT IS YOUR SERVICE

"Wives, be subject to your own Husbands, as [a service] to the Lord." It's a short verse, but it is very, very powerful. We may think that this scripture is saying that to any person outside of our marriage. (Ephesians 5:22).

My Husband is mine! "But let's look at the second part of the above verse. It says, "As a service unto the Lord." It is a service unto the Lord to undergird your Husband and pray, to be subject to your Husband, to be submitted to your Husband. It's okay to be strong and still submit. Being a submitted woman is nothing to be ashamed of. People often view being submissive or holding onto a marriage as a sign of weakness. Let me say for the record, if you haven't stood for a marriage that is falling apart, you have no idea how much strength it takes. Fighting to preserve my marriage is the most difficult thing I have ever done, and it requires courage, strength, and supernatural intervention. Others have no concept of how challenging it truly is to maintain a marriage. But God is ushering in a new era for women. He's initiating a fresh movement in relationships and families, and we are determined not to let go.

God declares in Isaiah 43:19: "Listen carefully, I am about to do a new thing, Now it will spring forth; Will you not be aware of it? I will even put a road in the wilderness, Rivers in the desert."

We are not going to let the enemy destroy our relationships and our families.

When our Husbands get delivered, our children can get delivered.

We stand for our families.

We stand for what God stands for.

We know that marriage is a covenant.

We know we have to do what God says and we will not get weary in well doing.

Wives, your Helpmeet role is a service unto the Lord. But it may feel more comfortable to say:

"My Husband doesn't deserve it. Do you know what he did? Do you know what he said? Do you know what he's been doing? Do you know what's been going on in my marriage and our family? Do you know he's addicted? Do you know he's been cheating? He's an adulterer!"

But it's not about what your Husband is doing; it's about what God ordained. Yes, that's going to hurt you. Yes, it's going to be difficult. Yes, it's something that causes an opening or even a feeling of rejection or abandonment. However, you can deal with that because the Word says, "If the Son sets you free, you will be free indeed" (John 8:36). God will provide the healing you need, but don't give up on your Husband. Don't give up on your future Husband.

Declare: "I am a Helpmeet Suitable!"

There is help available for every Helpmeet. Don't be ashamed to admit that you don't know how to do it or that you're uncertain about your role in the Kingdom. Your role is to stand up for your family. "Therefore, put on the full armor of God, so that when the day of evil comes, you may be able to stand your ground, and after you have done everything, to stand" (Ephesians 6:13). This is your service unto the Lord.

When you look at your Husband through your eyes and consider all that he has done, you might be inclined to say he doesn't deserve it. But does God deserve it? Given how good God has been to you, how He's been working in you, through you, and for you, He is worth the effort. He is worth your obedience to what He's asking you to do. He has asked you to stay and pray. He has asked you to undergird. He has asked you to help His son find deliverance. He has asked you to provide love and support to His son. He has asked you to treat your Husband like a King and help him grasp who God truly is through your actions and words.

Sometimes, we have to do things before we see the results. That's what faith is all about. In Hebrews 11:1, faith is defined as,

"Confidence in what we hope for and assurance about what we do not see." Faith isn't rooted in visible circumstances. It's rooted in what God has instructed you to do. If God has asked you to be sanctified, set apart, and holy in order to undergird your family and support your Husband until:

He gets that job that he needs

He understands that God truly loves him.

He gets off the street.

He gets off the drugs, alcohol, and/or pornography

He comes back home and understands his role—then your faithfulness to that calling is crucial.

Until these things happen, you stand on the Word, and you don't move. You stand on the Word, and you say, "God, heal me! God, support me! God, give me strength!" He will give you the strategies you need to stand firm. We know that women are strong, but when it comes to the household, all of a sudden, we act as if we can't stand or do it. I am a living witness—it is hard!—but it is worth it. We can do all things with the help of God. Ephesians 6:10 declares, "Finally, be strong in the Lord and in his mighty power" for we can do all things through Christ who strengthens us (Philippians 4:13). We say those scriptures, but it's time to stand and declare that we're strong in the Lord. We're strong enough to be helped. We must be strong enough for others to lean on us until they can stand on their own. That's what an assistant does—support. Assistants can be counted on to help. Can your Husband count on you? Can God count on you? Ephesians 5:22 reminds us that we are to do what God has asked us to do as a service to Him. God has done what He needs to do. If He asks us to help, He will give us the strength to do it. There is no limit to what we can do.

I'm a living witness. My Husband and I have seen a significant breakthrough. We've seen reconciliation. We've definitely seen healing. You can fight while you are healing. You can pray when you are healed. You can stand on the Word of God when you are healed. I know you are getting weary. But with healing, you can stand and keep running this race. Sometimes you say, "God, I can't do it!" But He's not asking you to do it in your own strength. He's asking you to do it in His strength. As it is written in Galatians 6:9, "Let us not become weary in doing good, for at the proper time we will reap a harvest if we do not give up."

Again, there is no limit to what God is going to do! You can, and you will sanctify your Husband, which will sanctify your family.

HELPMEET JOURNAL ENTRY

1. What is God saying to you after reading this chapter?
2. What are some prayer targets you need to add?

~

_____

_____

_____

_____

_____

_____

_____

_____

_____

_____

_____

_____

_____

_____

_____

_____

_____

_____

_____

_____

_____

12

A SANCTIFIED WIFE'S PRAYERS

WRITE THE VISION AND MAKE IT PLAIN

While on my journey of becoming a Helpmeet Suitable, God taught me strategic ways to decree and declare my Husband's destiny. Then He asked me to continue to decree, even when circumstances looked as if they were headed in the wrong direction. God asked me to declare my Husband's purpose and calling consistently, even when it didn't coincide with what I was speaking. Trust me—I know how hard it is to speak over your spouse when it seems he is doing his own thing and couldn't care less about anything but himself. The battle for my marriage went back and forth for about 8-10 years. The first 4 years were challenging because I didn't see any fruit from my prayers. However, as time went by, God impressed upon my heart to do more than pray. God asked me to decree and declare my Husband's destiny over him consistently.

God led me to read and meditate on Habakkuk 2:2: "Write down the revelation and make it plain on tablets so that a herald may run with it."

Quickly, I realized I hadn't written any of my decrees and declarations about my Husband. As a Helpmeet Suitable, I encourage you to commit to writing or typing your decrees because you may forget. The devil is cunning and crafty (Genesis 3:1), so he will start to burden your mind with thoughts outside of God's will. He will remind you of your emotional pain and try to discourage you.

The Holy Spirit prompted me to stop praying based on my emotions. For example, I would say, "God, do this, fix Gerald, and bring us back together." My prayers were more of a complaint than a declaration.

The Lord said, "You need to act like a soldier! You are in a war, a battle for your Husband's life, for his destiny, and your children's lifestyle! This battle is about your household!" So, I changed my posture in prayer. I declared that my Husband is a Priest, Prophet, and King of our home, a man of God, and the leader of our family, the head of our household" (1 Corinthians 11:3).

As you read and prepare for this assignment as your Husband's Helpmeet Suitable, think about your responses to the following questions:

•What are your Husband's roles?

•What are some of the things that your Husband is called to do?

•What are some of the things your Husband should be doing?

DECREE THE WORD

Once I learned how to specifically decree and declare these statements about Gerald out loud and consistently, God instructed me to write what the Bible said about my Husband and include the scriptures in plain language. For example, years ago, an apostle walked over to Gerald and me and said that we have a ministry of reconciliation. So, I wrote down that Gerald is a minister of reconciliation. Then, I looked up scriptures that had to do with reconciliation and found 2 Corinthians 5:18, which says, "All things are of God, who has reconciled us to Himself by Jesus Christ and has given us a ministry of reconciliation." Combining the scripture with the prophetic word that was spoken about Gerald elevated my faith to another level. I would decree the gift Gerald had and recite the prophetic message that was spoken, but what gave my efforts more strength was actually associating a scripture with it.

Next, the Lord told me to find resources related to the prophecies and decrees spoken about Gerald. God led me to read books on leadership. I studied the chapters and wrote a specific statement from the books with Gerald's name in it. This allowed me to declare that Gerald has a ministry of reconciliation according to the Scriptures and the Christian books God led me to read. Gerald has received prophecies that even said he would give birth to prophets. I took that prophetic word and stood on it by speaking it forth. Assembling these pieces gave me strength. Following these instructions also helped me get out of my emotions. I stopped worrying about what was happening around me because as I fixed my focus on the Word and declarations, my perspective changed.

Throughout this battle, God reminded me that I wouldn't see the results of my prayers instantly, but I needed to make declarations as if I saw my prayers answered. I had to believe it and then I would see it! The Lord also told me not to concern myself with what people said, what I saw, or Gerald's behavior because focusing on any of these things would lead to discouragement. During that period, we had been separated several times, and things didn't look as if they would ever improve. Despite this, God instructed me to continue to decree and declare over my Husband. It was difficult, but I also knew God is faithful.

MY HUSBAND IS A KING

You might be thinking, "I've never received a prophecy, and my Husband hasn't been in situations to receive prophecies." In that case, you can begin by searching the Word of God and start speaking what God says about your Husband. All Husbands are meant to be Priests, Prophets, and Kings of their homes. Look up scriptures that help you honor your Husband as the leader and King. This doesn't imply that your Husband holds the official title of a Prophet, but all of us are called to prophesy, specifically, a Husband is the Prophet of his family.

I also read several books about being a Kingdom man because I desired my Husband to exhibit the qualities, characteristics, and lifestyle of a Kingdom man. I recommend you search for scriptures about a Kingdom man and a Kingdom Husband. Start declaring that your Husband is a Kingdom man and a Kingdom father. You can begin with 1 Timothy 3:4-5. Speaking the Word of God provides assurance and will help you stand firm. The Bible tells us that if one spouse can hold on and remain righteous, believing in the Word and speaking it, it can influence the other spouse to seek Christ.

Another scripture you can declare over your Husband is Matthew 6:33. Declare that your spouse is a man who seeks the Kingdom of

God and His righteousness first, and trusts that all these things will be added unto him.

WHAT DOES THE WORD OF GOD SAY?

Don't become discouraged if your Husband isn't part of a church or an environment where prophecies are common. Rely on what God's Word says about him. Declare that your Husband is a man of God. Have faith in the Holy Spirit, as there are insights the Holy Spirit will reveal to you about your Husband.

When I began this process, I was reading, studying, declaring, and decreeing through tears, pain, and hurt. I asked God for more strength, and He provided it. Consistently decreeing what the Bible says about your Husband will prevent the enemy from obstructing both of you. Always trust and speak the identity God assigns to your Husband. I also encourage you to speak over your Husband's career and business endeavors. As we work on restoring, speaking, decreeing, and declaring, it will be established (Job 22:28). Trust and believe that this strategy sets forth God's promises into the atmosphere.

Another prophecy spoken over my Husband is that he has an entrepreneurial anointing. I instilled into the atmosphere what Gerald was created to accomplish. At the same time, I resisted my thoughts about how he was behaving. I had to remember that the enemy was operating through him, and his actions did not truly represent who God had created him to be. I had to look beyond what I saw and rely on what God said. That's the true test of faith! Faith is the substance of things hoped for and the evidence of things not seen (Hebrews 11:1). While we might notice certain things in our spouses, those traits aren't in line with who God said they are. Thus, we choose to decree and declare. We must stand on the Word, and when we stand on the Word and declare it, we must believe it to be so.

CHANGE THE WAY YOU SEE HIM

In the very beginning, you might find it tough to believe, so it's crucial to write the vision down and make it plain. After my Husband and I began communicating again, I started texting and emailing the decrees to him. Over time, this practice has become a routine that aids him in maintaining his deliverance. As I decreed and declared over my Husband, something incredible happened: it changed me. It transformed my mindset regarding who I was speaking to and what I was saying about my Husband.

I encourage you to ask yourself: who am I living with? Who am I married to? You will gradually come to realize that your Husband is a King. He is a Prophet. He is a child of God, and you must treat him in accordance with what God said, no matter the circumstances. Treat your Husband as the blessing he is. When you can decree throughout the day that your Husband is a Priest, Prophet, and King, you will shift how you perceive him and, ultimately, how you treat him.

For example, decree and declare:

- My Husband is the leader of our home.
- My Husband is wealthy, and he leaves a legacy for our children.
- My Husband is a Kingdom father.

Continuing to make these declarations will change the way you speak to your spouse. I began conversing with Gerald in a manner that was far more respectful, gentle, and loving because I could perceive him through God's eyes. My compassion grew, and my words initiated a transformation within our home. Small beginnings should not be belittled; even if you're declaring just one or two things with strength and conviction, do it. Then, allow the Holy Spirit to guide you toward new strategies. A few weeks into this assignment, the Holy Spirit prompted me to declare, "Gerald is a modern-day David." Initially, I didn't grasp the full meaning of this statement, but I was resolved not to reject the Holy Spirit's guidance and be disobedient. So, I researched some of David's attributes and spoke those qualities over Gerald. Avoid becoming overly engrossed in the details—instead, let the Holy Spirit lead you. The Holy Spirit might reveal that your spouse is meant to be a worship leader or to minister to young men. Your Husband could be called to address vast audiences.

The scripture God directed me to was that David was "a man after God's own heart" (Acts 13:22). Gerald's behavior during that time didn't fall in line with someone who was after God's own heart. Similarly, David's lifestyle in no way resembled his eventual accomplishments and identity. David's early life was marred by corruption, including lust and perversion. David had no true understanding of who he was; yet, the Word of God affirms that he was "a man after God's own heart." So, who are we to question God? I had to stop saying, "Is this really the person You want to use? Are You sure?" God, in His compassion, assured me that He created Gerald to lead, help, serve others, and save souls. As my comprehension of God and His Word deepened, I could perceive Gerald as God saw him.

SOLDIERS USE STRATEGIES

There is incredible strength in speaking the Word of God. Even the Bible says we can speak to a mountain and that mountain will be removed (Mark 11:23). Decreeing is definitely not something I could have come up with on my own, nor was it something I felt like doing. But now I see it coming to pass. I see Gerald coming forward and being molded into exactly who God created him to be. I see him walking out his salvation and deliverance in a genuine way. Decreeing will cause you to become a soldier. No soldier goes to war without a plan or strategy. Decreeing is a strategy that says, "Devil, you cannot have my spouse. You cannot have his destiny. You cannot have his purpose. I believe strongly that this person is worth fighting for. This is a child of God. This is a son of God. This person has a purpose, not only in my life but in the lives of the people they're supposed to touch. So, I'm going to fight for that person!"

Please don't give up. I know it's tough. I know it's hard. It seemed impossible my Husband would change because of his addictions, lifestyle, behavior, and attitude. Oh, but if you could see where he is now! I'm so thankful that God delivered my Husband and reconciled our relationship. Our life together is getting better every day. Helpmeets, I encourage you to ask the Holy Spirit, "What strategy should I use, God? I'm a soldier, and I'm committed to what I'm doing." If your marriage is strong, I encourage you to do this before there's an issue because decreeing who your Husband is and where your family is headed is your ministry. This is speaking to the mountaintops. This is not something you do for about a week, see no tangible results, shrug your shoulders, and give up by saying, "Maybe it worked for her, but it's not working for me."

Let me be clear—decreeing and speaking over my Husband was not something I did for a week. This is something I do as a part of my lifestyle because gifts and callings are without repentance (Romans 11:29). I don't want my Husband to start operating in his gifts and then fall. I continue with this same strategy. There are times when I go back to my list because the Holy Spirit may want me to start speaking more about something. So, I'll study that particular calling in his life. Sometimes I look back and ask God, "Is there something specific you want me to say?" Then, when I go to bed, I put my hand on Gerald's head, and I start speaking who he is. And that's just how we do it. Gerald does not struggle when I pray for him at night anymore. He loves it. My Husband loves it so much that when I pray for him, he asks me to pray for other things. That's the way God wants it to be. Sometimes I wake up now, and my Husband's praying over me. I feel so good because that's what I do for him. Now I'm able to not only see the prayers come to life but experience my Husband strategically praying for me in the same way.

PRAYER FOR STRENGTH AND CONSISTENCY

Father God, in the name of Jesus, I thank You that I am a Helpmeet who presses toward the mark of the high calling. Thank You, Father, for giving me strategies to fight because You have called me to be a soldier in Your army. You have given me physical and mental strength and ability over all the powers of the enemy. Where I am weak, Lord, You are strong. I am thankful that I can run to You and find safety. I thank You, Father God, because You are a strong tower. I decree and declare I will not get weary in well-doing. I can do all things through You because You give me strength. I will not slow down or stop fighting for my family. I speak to the mountain of confusion or dysfunction in my relationship and say it is removed and cast into the sea. Anything out of Your will is canceled now. I thank and praise You, Lord God, that You have given me authority over all powers of the enemy. I believe Your Word is quick and powerful and sharper than any two-edged sword. We are thanking You, Father God, that our spouses and children are saved, set free, delivered, and doing the will of God in every area of their lives. They will not fall. They will not falter. They will not stop. Father God, I thank You that my family is growing from level to level, glory to glory, and we are operating in our gifts and callings. All these things I ask. In Jesus' name. Amen.

HELPMEET JOURNAL ENTRY

1. What is God saying to you after reading this chapter?
2. What are some prayer targets you need to add?

~

_____

_____

_____

_____

_____

_____

_____

_____

_____

_____

_____

_____

_____

_____

_____

_____

_____

_____

_____

_____

_____

_____

_____

_____

HELPMEET APPENDIX

ASSIGNMENT

As we conclude this book, I want you to take some time and create an Honor Vision. What does that vision look like? God's Word says (in Habakkuk 2:2) to write the vision and make it plain. Many of us are struggling with a lack of honor. Some of us may not know how to give honor or lack the skills to do so. This assignment is part of your homework. Listen to what God is asking of you. You will need to invest time in listening to what God is saying. You'll have to practice the necessary steps to put it into action. I encourage you to engage in role-playing, whether you're looking in the mirror, driving in your car, doing chores around the house, or whatever you're occupied with. Practice what honor sounds like and how to respond differently. We must practice what we desire to see; it doesn't happen suddenly.

The next aspect of your assignment is to study the scriptures that we reviewed in the chapters and ask God to reveal their meaning. Let's transform the way we express honor by staying immersed in the Word of God. Evaluate the way you speak and respond from God's perspective as you meditate on the scriptures concerning our role as Helpmeets. Allocate time to listen to what God is asking and guiding you toward. This might be challenging, but I urge you to prioritize considering your Husband's perspective in everything. If you're not married yet, seek God for what He wants you to consider in this regard. Dedicate 30 minutes to an hour every day for the next two weeks and zero in on this task. Seek God for His instructions. Ask God to reveal the areas where you haven't honored your Husband, and if you're not married, inquire where you might be missing a level of honor as you prepare for your future Husband. Immerse yourself in the scriptures and reflect on them; study to show yourself approved. When our mindsets change, God will shift things, so be attuned to feedback from the Holy Spirit as you delve into these scriptures and seek His guidance.

ASSIGNMENT

The next assignment is to journal what God is speaking to you concerning all that you are meditating on. As God begins to show you things, you should write them down. While journaling, listen to what God is saying and process these scriptures; it will begin to take root deep within your spirit. We need to seek deeper revelations and establish a foundation so that we begin to behave in a way that reflects our understanding of the role of the Helpmeet.

ASSIGNMENT

The final assignment for you is to do whatever you feel is necessary to sanctify yourself. This is an individual journey, so you will need to determine what is required for you on your path. Whether it's fasting or whatever you need, through this process, you will start to shift your thinking on how ministry is approached. Our goal is to perceive things from God's perspective. I am excited for you to embrace the Helpmeet role that you have been created for as your mindset begins to shift to align with the way God intended it!

ASSIGNMENT

Take 30 minutes each day and ask God to reveal more to you about how you can accomplish His plan for you specifically as a Helpmeet. During these 30 minutes, you should be listening to God and asking Him how to accomplish His plan—not your plan, not your will, but His. He is such a good Father. When I started asking God what He wanted, it was difficult in the beginning and it felt terrible. But when I truly got it, I realized as I began doing what God wanted, everything I desired was already in Him. I started seeing Him do things I had asked for and desired because He gives us the desires of our hearts (Psalm 37:4). When we pursue God's will, He takes care of us—He even provides things we don't ask for or know we want. This assignment is not simple, and I still work tirelessly to do it. It won't always be what you like or at the time you want.

ASSIGNMENT

Slow down and ask God to reveal more about how you can accomplish His plan, then start writing it down. When God begins to share insights with you, avoid trying to figure it out on your own. Don't think about how you're going to afford it or how many other things you have on your agenda. When those thoughts arise, shut them down. Listen to God's plan as it's tailored specifically for you as a Helpmeet. I encourage you to apply the same approach to other aspects of your life as well.

ASSIGNMENT

Write in your journal daily what you hear God saying. Try your best to set aside your own desires so you can genuinely hear God. Simply write. Later, go back and review what you have written. Make sure to date your journal entries.

ASSIGNMENT

Write your own personal honor agreement to God and your King using scriptures. This process consists of two parts. Part one involves writing an honor agreement to God, where you've decided to agree with Him to honor His will and His Word. Search for scriptures in the Bible and craft an agreement to obediently follow God and His ways.

Part two, whether you're married or aspiring to be, write an honor agreement to your King or the King God has for you. Address it to your current Husband/current King or your future Husband/future King, depending on your situation. Write an honor agreement based on the scriptures you've studied. Use phrases like "I agree to" or "I promise to" and direct them toward your King. However, refrain from sharing it with him. This is something you must internalize in your spirit. Write this agreement to have a reference for what you've committed to according to scripture. If you don't find any scripture in your agreement upon reading it, identify appropriate scriptures and include them in accordance with God's Word. The core of this exercise is honor.

Read the scriptures from each chapter daily. Eventually, memorize them because, in challenging times, you'll need them. You will need God's Word to come forth from your spirit and be spoken out loud, enabling you to declare to satan and your flesh, "It is written." These scriptures need to become deeply rooted in your spirit and soul. That is achieved through consistent reading and study. I encourage you to recite them aloud as faith is strengthened through hearing. Read them daily. I also recommend recording and listening to them every day. These scriptures are essential to the Helpmeet role so invest time in familiarizing yourself with them. Remember this role is about God's will, God's Word, and God's way.

ASSIGNMENT

Evaluate

Do an honest self-evaluation. It is key! Ask God to search you, and watch your emotions when you do. Ask yourself, "How am I doing?" Don't beat yourself up with your answer. Don't feel condemned when the Word convicts you because God corrects those He loves. When you strive to be a Helpmeet, you will discover how much God loves you as He will correct you. As you ask God and self-evaluate, write down what is revealed.

Needs Assessment

Ask yourself what resources, tools, information, and adjustments you need to make in order to implement God's plan. Identify your needs and then put the work in. God will lead you to the right resources necessary for His plan for you as His daughter. When we take the time to assess, God will guide us. This Helpmeet role is not only about marriage; it's about God's perfect will and understanding why He created us and what He placed inside us.

I was able to see God as a deliverer, healer, and provider through the Helpmeet role. I could hear His voice more clearly, and I began to mature in studying. But to do this, I needed resources, tools, and information, and I had to make adjustments. I didn't gather everything all at once; I followed a plan and saw improvements. I'm still following the plan and acquiring resources. I'm still studying and gaining revelation and insight from God. I'm shifting as a Helpmeet and a daughter. I'm shifting in this Deborah season, and it's ongoing. It's necessary. Seek God on how to obtain the resources you need for your purpose and evaluate everything in your life.

There was a time in my life when I was separated from my Husband and losing my house to foreclosure. I was facing trying times, but God told me what to study and what books to buy; he worked it out every time. He guided me to where to sow financially and then blessed me with favor as a result of my obedience. I changed my mindset. I shifted from thinking that I couldn't do it to believing if God said it, He would provide. It was not easy, but God provided! It was difficult, but would I do it again? Absolutely. Would I want to do it again? Not at all, but I would if it were required as part of God's will.

Now, I see such an amazing difference in my whole family. My children are shifting and changing. My Husband is growing in his assignment, destiny, purpose, and role because that was God's perfect will.

COMMON CONCERNS AND QUESTIONS

"There may be times God asks us to temporarily cover other responsibilities, am I expected to do both?"

The answer to this is yes. There may be times when God asks you to temporarily cover other responsibilities, such as your King's responsibility as a father or something else. Remember, we talked about how a sanctified wife can sanctify her Husband, so you have to tell the devil you're sanctifying your spouse and you will stand in the gap and intercede. You will do what's necessary and allow God to use you because Jesus took your place. Jesus took responsibility for our sins on the cross, and He is our example. So yes, there may be times when God will ask something of you for a time that will help get your family, your King, and your destiny from point A to point B.

As a mother, because you have many duties, you may ask your oldest child to clean up after your youngest. The child may get upset, wondering why he has to clean up after his younger sibling, but it's because he is the oldest, and Mommy needs his help. God may do this at times as well, just as we do it often as parents. It's temporary. Sometimes we see God in a bad light when He asks us to do things, but we do it as parents, and it is no different. There are times parents will ask children to do something for their siblings until the siblings can do it for themselves. Yes, there are things that a Husband is supposed to do, but you let God deal with your Husband concerning that.

"If I'm doing all of this, what is my Husband (King) doing?"

If you study the Husband's role, you will see he has plenty to do. Satan attacks the Husband more strongly because he is strategic enough to know if he conquers the head, certain things will never be in place. Husbands succumb to many challenges because people don't know how to help them address the issues they face. We are now in a culture where many men are out of their roles and lack understanding because they are under attack by the enemy, and they don't know how to respond. Many families are struggling because they do not know what to do. Many generations have lacked proper guidance, and we are witnessing the results of that now. While it's not God's will for us to be in this situation, He will provide us with the blueprint to overcome it. However, this requires our obedience and suitability. We must submit ourselves to God's will so He can guide us. As Helpmeets, we already have enough to work on, so let's focus on that instead of dwelling on what our Kings are not doing.

"When will my needs or desires be fulfilled?"

That's a good question, and it's valid. However, nobody can give you the answer to that question except God, so you will need to ask yourself if you are willing to give up your needs and desires to fulfill your destiny. Talk to God about it. Are you willing to deny yourself to take up your cross and follow God? I'm not saying He won't give you the desires of your heart because He will, but sometimes the desires of our hearts don't line up with God's perfect will and we have to become mature enough to pursue it. God's perfect will already has our needs in mind but sometimes some things have to happen prior to our needs being fulfilled, so we have to align with His will first. God is a good Father and His desire is to make sure our needs are met and our desires are fulfilled.

It's similar to times when we may have to sow a seed to get out of poverty. Sometimes, it is just part of the process. If we focus on our desires and needs being met, we will hop around and do all sorts of different things, trying to fulfill those needs and desires. We will ultimately end up fulfilling our flesh and be outside of His will. Our needs are on God's mind but not before someone's salvation or deliverance.

"This is too much...why would God ask this of me?"

Let's reflect on Jesus Christ at the cross and understand there is nothing God has asked us to do that even comes close to what He asked of His Son. Nothing compares. If He asked His Son to do far more than He asked us to do, how can we let this question simmer in our hearts? Sacrifice is an integral part of the journey, but it purifies and delivers us. It matures and shapes us into vessels. Sacrifice makes us suitable for God's use. Every aspect of the refining fire transforms you into pure gold, so allow it to refine you. It equips us to be effective evangelists and leaders.

When we decide that it's simply too much, and we question why God would ask certain things of us, it's because He requires our deliverance and freedom. He demands our obedience. He desires us to follow His Word. Christianity is about following Christ. God asked Christ to die, and in the same way, we are asked to die to our flesh. We shouldn't complain about how challenging it is and walk away. Examine what God has asked of you and compare it to what Jesus Christ suffered and was asked to bear on our behalf. I encourage you to place your trust in God throughout the process.

HELPMEET SUITABLE PRAYERS

Father, I thank You for Scripture, which tells me to hide Your Word in my heart so I do not sin against You. God, I am committed to hiding Your Word in my heart. I'm committed to studying to show myself approved. I'm committed to rightly dividing the Word of Truth and understanding Your Word to increase my faith. I am committed to understanding through Your Word why You created my Husband and me and what You created us to do. I understand the role You created me for and the importance of being a good Helpmeet. I understand the significance of operating in the Helpmeet role so that my Priest, Prophet, and King can get the assistance he needs to operate in his role to do the will of God, what You have created both of us to do, and to cover and lead our family well.

I thank You, Lord, that I have understanding and wisdom as my principal things. God, in all of my getting, I am decreeing and declaring I shall understand this role. I shall understand Your will. I will not be conformed to this world but will be transformed by the daily renewing of my mind. Lord, completely renew my mind so it shifts, I desire Your Word, and I long to be all You have created us to be. I will not miss or lack anything. I will not just operate in the things I want to do, but I will operate in all the areas You have created for me. I don't want to miss anything that will please You. I desire everything You want for me and my Husband.

God, I decree and declare this is our season of things happening so fast that our heads will swim one thing fast on the heels of the other. I thank You, Lord God, that blessings upon blessings are coming. Favor upon favor is coming to us. But God, because of that, we must have the foundation of Your Word. I must have the foundation of understanding this Helpmeet role. God, give me the strength and healing I need. I'm asking for a supernatural desire, and I permit you to give me a hunger and thirst for righteousness. I have a hunger and thirst for You and Your will. I hunger for Your Word and Your way.

Forgive me for any time I was disobedient. Forgive me for any time I was not fervent because I know Your Word reminds me that the effectual, fervent prayers of the righteous Helpmeet avail much. I decree and declare that I will avail much as I understand this role, as I understand Your will, as I understand Your instructions, and as I understand Your precepts. I will not be moved by what other people do or say. I will not be moved by my situation and circumstances. God, keep my mind fastened to Your will and Your Word, and when it gets difficult, give me supernatural strength and peace. When it gets challenging, I want to hear Your voice, and a stranger's voice I will not follow. The stranger's voice is mute. In the name of Jesus.

I will do what You have asked me to do. I will do what You have called me to do. I declare that I am a Helpmeet Suitable, and I am operating in Your will and accomplishing all that You have created me to achieve. I ask all these things. In Jesus' name. There is no backlash or retaliation. Nothing is missing or lacking. I am the Helpmeet that You can count on and I shall be the wife who will sanctify my Husband. In Jesus' name. Amen.

PRAYER

Father God, I thank You for Your insight and revelation concerning this Helpmeet role as a lifestyle. God, give me direction for Your perfect will concerning my life. Give me supernatural power to walk in all that You have for me. I decree and declare an increase right now! In the name of Jesus. Increase in healing, resources, and revelation. Lord, I cancel every assignment that will cause me to feel I cannot carry out what You've instructed me to do because Your Word says that I can do all things through Christ who strengthens me, so I receive the strength of Christ to carry out Your will. I receive the strength of Christ to do what You have created me to do.

Thank You, God, for the honor of teaching me and creating me to be a Helpmeet Suitable. Anything that is in Your perfect will is a perfect plan, and I receive that perfect plan. God, I ask for forgiveness for any time I've complained about Your will. I ask forgiveness for any time I thought my will was greater than Your will or where I've thought that my plan was greater than Your plan. God, forgive me now. In the name of Jesus. Thank You for being such a forgiving God and that You forgive me and cast my wrong as far as the East is from the West. I am thankful for Your forgiveness.

Lord, give me understanding as I study to show myself approved. I will not move to the left or the right. I am going to press toward the mark of the high calling of God. I decree and declare that I am adaptable and complementary. I submit my spouse to You and I submit my will to You. I am submitted to Your Word and I declare not my will but Yours be done. You are a good Father and You will never leave us or forsake us. You will not hurt us in any way. I thank You, Lord, that I embrace Your plan and Your will. I will hide Your Word in my heart so I don't sin against You. Give me the understanding and the revelation to continuously pursue Your perfect plan, God. I will not be conformed to this world, but I will be transformed by the renewing of my mind so that I may prove what is the good, acceptable, and perfect will of God for my life.

I will adapt myself to my Husband, and I will submit. I am strong in You, Lord, and in the power of Your might, so give me the strength I need. Supernatural strength is coming into my life now. Even when I think I can't do it, I thank You, God, that You give me a boost in the spirit. In the name of Jesus. I will not give up. I will not shrink back. I will not slow down and, Lord, I will see miracles, signs, and wonders. I will continually see my marriage increase. I will continually see my children blessed. I will continually see myself as healthy and wealthy. I will see myself in Your divine will, God, because I am serving You. God, I understand that my Priest, Prophet, and King will benefit from me serving You. My children will benefit from it. My bloodline will benefit from it.

I decree that my prayers will be answered and I will see all of my children blessed and highly favored. I will see my marriage operating in the supernatural and perfect plan of God that was meant for us. In the mighty name of Jesus, I pray. Amen.

PRAYER

Father, in the name of Jesus, I thank You for forgiving me. I thank You for the opportunity to ask for Your forgiveness. I enter Your gates with thanksgiving and Your courts with praise. I am thankful for You and bless Your mighty name. Thank You, Father, for giving me the authority to put on the whole armor of God as I cancel things in the spirit realm. I need protection from the tricks and schemes of the enemy. You've given me authority in Your Word to cover myself under the blood of Jesus so I put on the whole armor of God. Weapons may come but they will not prosper. I have the helmet of salvation, the breastplate of righteousness, the gospel of peace on my feet, and the belt of truth around me. I have the sword of the Spirit in one hand and the shield of faith in the other hand. You are my rear guard and You cover me, Lord. Regardless of what I see, I will believe You and keep on believing. Open the eyes of my understanding and increase my faith. Lord, cancel any hope deferred that is trying to make the heart sick. I will hope and keep on hoping. I will stand and keep on standing. In the name of Jesus.

I will not stop or back down from God's assignment for my life. I will press toward the mark of the high calling in Christ Jesus. Thank You for blessing my marriage, my children, and my bloodline. I refuse to allow the assignment of the enemy in my life and I stop it before it touches my children. I thank You, Father, and I utilize the authority and power of Christ over all powers of the enemy. I believe in Your Word and that You created me to help. I will not operate as a hindrance. If I have operated as a hindrance in the past, God, forgive me. You have forgiven me and cast my sins as far as the East is from the West so I will not bring them up because You won't bring them up. I will not be condemned, and I crush every condemning spirit now. I will not be condemned for the things I did not know or understand. I will not be condemned for the mistakes I have made. From now on and moving forward, I will do what Your Word says. God, I thank You that I am more disciplined in the spirit. I will read and study Your Word and hide it in my heart so I do not sin against You.

I command the spirit of strength to come over my life. I decree that I am strong in You, Lord, and in the power of Your might. Your might is directing and covering me. Your might is leading me in this Helpmeet role. I need Your strength so that I will not get weary in well-doing. I decree that I will stand firm in You, Lord. My marriage is aligned with the will of God and because I operate in the Helpmeet role, I will also cover my King. I will honor and respect him. I will assist him as You have called me to. I will be good help. I declare that I am a Titus Chapter 2 woman. It's an assignment and sacred service so I will raise up Helpmeets who are disciplined in the Lord and understand their biblical role in the family. I will raise up Helpmeets who aren't afraid of the enemy and know not only their role but their posture, not only their posture but their authority and power. In the mighty name of Jesus. The curse we have seen before we will see no more. I believe Your Word. In Jesus' name. Amen.

PRAYER

Father God, in the name of Jesus, I am honored You have called me a Helpmeet. I declare I will strive to be a representation of the Holy Spirit to my family. Please forgive me for things I have done to work against You and for anything that was not pleasing according to Your Word. I know You are a forgiving God, so I leave those thoughts, actions, and behaviors in the past. Thank You for sending me the Holy Spirit to guide me to be the best Helpmeet for my Husband (future Husband). Lord, give me strategies, wisdom, insight, and strength to do what You have called me to do. If I fall short, Lord, help me to get back up quickly. I declare I will not fall, but I will stand firm. I declare I am growing level to level and glory to glory. I know that life and death are in the power of my tongue, so I speak life to my marriage, ministry, family, purpose, and destiny. I will shift with You, Father. I declare I am a comforter, advocate, intercessor, strengthener, and counselor. Make me a suitable, adaptable, trainable, and accommodating Helpmeet. In the name of Jesus. Amen.

PRAYER

Father God, in the name of Jesus, develop me into a Helpmeet Suitable. God, You have called for me to be complementary. You have called for me to stand alongside my Husband. Teach me, Father God, Your will and Your way. Download information into me so that I know exactly what You want for my marriage and my family. I thank You, Lord God, that You are teaching me to line up my life with Your Word. Help me to keep my mouth closed when You ask me and to declare when You tell me. Help me to listen and be still when You tell me to be still and to know and understand my role in the household. I thank You, Lord God, that I am pushing my Husband forward and not pulling him back. I will always do Your will. Create in me a clean heart, oh God, and renew a right spirit within me. I use my authority to cancel every assignment of pain, hurt, past trauma, and things that have happened to me in former relationships that I may have brought into my marriage. I declare right now that my family is free. We are set free from all generational curses. Lord God, You have called me to help, and I refuse to hinder my Husband. Help me to respect and honor him in a way that pleases You. God, download the information into me so that I will know exactly how to love him unconditionally and forgive him continually, as You have loved and forgiven me.

Father God, Heal my heart from any negative experiences. Heal the pain that I have when I feel rejected or abandoned. In the name of Jesus. I cancel any trauma from my childhood. In the name of Jesus.

I thank You, Lord God, that as You heal me, I can speak Your Word boldly over my Husband. I declare I have created an atmosphere that's conducive to deliverance in our home. I am standing on Your Word and declaring that I am a Helpmeet Suitable. When the enemy steps in, Father, lift a standard against him. You have given me the authority to tread on, trample upon, and stomp down every serpent and scorpion. Father, thank You for physical and mental strength and the ability to cast down all powers of the enemy that come against my Husband, my destiny, or my purpose. In the name of Jesus, I take authority over everything that tries to come against us. I am a Helpmeet Suitable, created by God, especially for my Husband.

Create in me a clean heart and teach me to hear Your still, small voice. Father, teach me what You want to teach me so that I can carry out Your will in our home. Teach me to be kind with my words as I use them to elevate, affirm, and encourage my Husband. I declare that he always feels loved unconditionally and respected. Please forgive me for the times I was angry, unforgiving, and upset.

I thank You, Lord, that as I embrace my role as a Helpmeet, I will be used in a mighty way. Equip me with supernatural strength to overcome the enemy and the strength to continue this journey. In Jesus' name. Amen.

DECLARATIONS FOR THE HELPMEET SUITABLE

I believe strongly in declaring the Word because there's power in our words. If you're writing it and claiming it, tell the devil "You might have gotten me down once, but you're not getting me down again. I'm getting back up. I'm getting up bigger and stronger, and I'm going to be rooted in the Word. I am rooted in the things of God. And I'm going to do what God has called me to do." Declare it today, and never stop declaring, "I am ..."

I am a Helpmeet Suitable.
I am submissive.
I honor my Husband.
I respect my Husband.
I build my Husband up.
I am his advocate.
I am an intercessor.
I am a sanctified wife.
I complement my Husband.
I am one with my Husband.

I bring peace to my Husband.
I am faithful to my Husband.
I will not hinder my Husband.
I am my Husband's "safe place."
I love my Husband unconditionally.
I pray for my Husband unceasingly.
I stand by and help my Husband.
I believe what God says about my Husband.
I know and support my Husband's calling.
I war in the spirit on behalf of my Husband.
I support my Husband's dreams and endeavors.
I believe in God's perfect will for my Husband.
I will not be used by the enemy against my Husband.
My home is conducive to deliverance.
My words will be Holy Spirit-led and edifying.

Helpmeet Resources

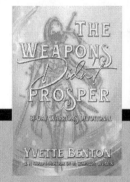 

Purchase books at

geraldandyvette.com or

amazon.com.

Join the Helpmeet Army mentoring program at geraldandyvette.com.

Take online courses at helpmeetu.com.

BIBLIOGRAPHY

1. *NAS Exhaustive Concordance of the Bible with Hebrew-Aramaic and Greek Dictionaries.* Copyright © 1981, 1998 by The Lockman Foundation. All rights reserved. Lockman.org.

2. Merriam-Webster. (n.d.). Helpmeet. In *Merriam-Webster.com dictionary*. Retrieved September 2, 2023, from https://www.merriam-webster.com/dictionary/helpmeet

3. *suitable, adj. & adv.* (July 2023). *Oxford English Dictionary*, Oxford University Press. https://doi.org/10.1093/OED/7440653108

4. Thayer's Greek Lexicon, Electronic Database. Copyright © 2002, 2003, 2006, 2011 by Biblesoft, Inc. All rights reserved. Used by permission. BibleSoft.com

ABOUT THE AUTHOR

Yvette Benton and her husband Gerald have been married for 23 years. God has called them to a unique team ministry using their personal testimonies of deliverance from addictions, separation, and financial struggles. Their transparency allows them to counsel and teach others that through Christ, faith, and hard work, God can and will heal marriages. They use their journey to reconciliation to help others understand that marriage works if you work it.

CONTACT YVETTE BENTON

Contact Yvette Benton on her various social media platforms:

www.GeraldandYvette.com

facebook.com/geraldandyvette

instagram.com/Helpmeet_Yvette

youtube.com/gym-geraldyvetteministries3210

Made in the USA
Middletown, DE
03 September 2024

60293431R00110